BLUE FASA

ALSO BY NATHANIEL MACKEY

Poetry Books and Chapbooks

Four for Trane
Septet for the End of Time
Outlantish
Song of the Andoumboulou: 18–20
Four for Glenn
Eroding Witness
School of Udhra
Whatsaid Serif
Splay Anthem
Nod House
Anuncio's Last Love Song
Outer Pradesh

Fiction

Bedouin Hornbook
Djbot Baghostus's Run
Atet A.D.
Bass Cathedral
From a Broken Bottle Traces of Perfume Still Emanate: Vols. 1–3

Criticism

*Discrepant Engagement: Dissonance, Cross-Culturality, and
  Experimental Writing*
Paracritical Hinge: Essays, Talks, Notes, Interviews

Anthologies

Moment's Notice: Jazz in Poetry and Prose, with Art Lange

Recordings

Strick: Song of the Andoumboulou 16–25

BLUE FASA

NATHANIEL MACKEY

A NEW DIRECTIONS BOOK

Some of these poems first appeared in the following publications: *African American Review, Ambush Review, Amerarcana: A Bird & Beckett Review, The American Reader, Blackbox Manifold, Broome Street Review, Caliban Online, Callaloo, Columbia, Conjunctions, From a Compos't, The Iowa Review, Island, Kadar Koli, Lana Turner, Lumina, Lumn, Manor House Quarterly, New American Writing, Poet Lore* and *The Poetry Project Newsletter.*

"A Night in Jaipur," "Stick City Bhajan," "Song of the Andoumboulou: 88," "Song of the Andoumboulou: 89," and "Moment's Gnosis" were published as a chapbook, *Outer Pradesh*, by Anomalous Press in 2014.

The author would like to thank the John Simon Guggenheim Memorial Foundation, whose award of a Fellowship for the year 2010–2011 contributed to the completion of this book.

Manufactured in the United States of America
New Directions Books are printed on acid-free paper
First published as a New Directions Paperbook (NDP1304) in 2015

Library of Congress Cataloging-in-Publication Data
Mackey, Nathaniel, 1947–
[Poems. Selections]
Blue Fasa / Nathaniel Mackey.
pages ; cm
ISBN 978-0-8112-2445-1 (softcover : acid-free paper)
I. Title.
PS3563.A3166A6 2015
811'.54—dc23   2014037946

10 9 8 7 6 5 4 3 2 1

ndbooks.com

New Directions Books are published for James Laughlin
by New Directions Publishing Corporation
80 Eighth Avenue, New York 10011

*to the memory of
my father
Alexander Obadiah Mackey
1915–1968*

Hoooh! Fasa!

    —The Dausi

    —Kenny Dorham, "Blue Bossa"

CONTENTS

II. RAG

Blue Fasa continues *Nod House*'s continuation of *Splay Anthem* and the work that came before it, braiding the two serial poems *Song of the Andoumboulou* and *"Mu."* It continues a long song that's one and more than one, "The / one song the songs all wanted in / on, all inwardness inside out. The / one song the songs, added or / not, added up to, song any one song / was," as "Song of the Andoumboulou: 68" puts it. The titles of its two sections, "Rāg" and "Rag," nearly rhyme and rhyme, respectively, with the title shared by *Nod House*'s two sections, "Quag," one index of the work's ongoingness. "Rāg," moreover, takes up a figure *Nod House*'s cross-cultural traverse arrives at and moves through in its penultimate poem, a figure signifying recursion and complaint: "Bone / we picked and picked at, ragalike picking / no / end." It announces an Eastern turn *Blue Fasa* picks up or picks at pronouncedly at the beginning, a thread it returns to throughout.

The sympathetic strings or the caught strings at Lakshmi's gaming table in the opening poem "A Night in Jaipur," the catch of the heart and the call of romance though they clearly are, are also the song itself, the poem itself, especially seriality itself. A sympathetic string on the sitar, the sarangi and other Indian instruments vibrates in response to a note played on the corresponding main string, sounding, by way of sympathetic resonance, the same note in unison or an octave above or below, or at an interval such as a fifth or a fourth away. It agrees with the note, feels with it, not without qualification or shades of difference in these latter cases, extending it, filling it out and allowing it to linger in doing so. Likewise, the long song, the long poem, particularly the serial poem, culls and extends a field of sympathetic resonances, lingering while moving on by way of recursiveness and feeling-with. To borrow a phrase from Rahsaan Roland Kirk (whose album *Boogie-Woogie String Along for Real* also pertains), it wants to be a vibration society. This has been and continues to be the practice of *Song of the Andoumboulou* and *"Mu."*

Such vibration brings multiple senses of string into play. It reminds us, for one, of something I've been unable to forget, that the root of the word *lyric* is the lyre, the musical instrument the ancient Greeks accompanied songs and recitations with. It's not that I've wanted to forget, though at times I've wondered if it were something I'd made up or been misinformed about, the lyric of late being so widely equated with phanopoetic snapshot, bare-bones narrative, terse epiphany and the like much more than with music, signaling an ongoing split between poetry and musicality perhaps. I also haven't been able to forget that for centuries poets in English have punned or played on *lyre*'s homophony with *liar*, suggesting an awareness of words' ability to mislead, a self-suspecting wariness we tend to arrogate to postmodernity. This I've in fact made an effort to forget, wanted to forget, wanting not always to be so wary as well as wanting not to remember that—contra one of our claims to originality even as we eschew originality—wariness and suspicion didn't just get here fifty or sixty years ago. Actually, I've wanted and not wanted to forget.

Poetry, to echo Louis Zukofsky, is an art whose lower limit is check, upper limit enchantment. Or is it upper limit check, lower limit enchantment? Poetry is the art of having both—horizontally or, if not, each variably above and below the other. Our recent turn toward promoting check over enchantment wants to forget *lyric*'s etymology, as though the art might arrive at a point where there were no strings attached. But strings are always attached, even in the most thoroughgoing doubt or disenchantment. Even check, itself a sort of string, knows that. What to do, then, if not pluck, bow, strum, scrape, scratch? The long song, the long poem, particularly the serial poem, the extended lyric, is one in which carol and qualm, carol and qualification, carol and caveat run as one. This is what Amiri Baraka heard in John Coltrane's "I Want to Talk about You" on the *Coltrane Live at Birdland* album: "instead of the simplistic though touching note-for-note replay of the ballad's line, on this performance each note is tested, given a slight tremolo or emotional vibrato (note to chord to scale reference), which makes it seem as if each one of the notes is given the possibility of 'infinite' qualification."

Pull is also what one can do, what one can succumb to. Among the Hofriyati, Janice Boddy's pseudonym for the inhabitants of a Sudanese village in her *Wombs and Alien Spirits: Women, Men, and the Zār Cult in Northern Sudan*, a book cited in the final poem in *Blue Fasa*'s first section, the trance-inducing chants of the *zār* possession ritual are called "threads" and when sung they are said to be "pulled." Pull is a mix of rapport and alterity, the call of dispersed or distended identity, perturbations attendant on feeling-with. It is the long song's call, the long poem's call, particularly the serial poem's or the extended lyric's invitation or call, pull that calls for an answering pull. Hofriyati women in seeking states of possession seek redress for disconsolate identity, a too tightly bound or tied up identity whose cords they seek to unloose. Pull is disjunctive sensibility's call, a dynamic in which undular and corpuscular senses of self meet and unravel, a play of dislocated identity, quantum gap, quantum tug, assets as well as losses redounding to tenuous extension. "I was possessed. I wasn't there" in "Hofriyati Head Opening" vibrates with "Insofar as there / was an I it wasn't hers" in "A Night in Jaipur" and with the Rasta-influenced coinage that enters the series, "Insofar-I," a coinage that runs claim and qualm as one, nomination and agnosis as one, proposing a subjunctive, qualified I, an alternate, unmortared I. Such a self, speaking or singing with a torn voice reminiscent of Lorca's *duende* or like Rumi's uprooted reed in the *Masnavi*, laments cosmic dislocation, social disability, sexual distress, and other afflictions. This is the Hofriyati "illness older than books" the book wants to get back to, as in the possibility of or the subjection to "'infinite' qualification" Baraka notes in Trane's playing or as in Wilson Harris's *Black Marsden*, where a character says of the "diary of infinity" he keeps, "My book is not autobiographical. I lose myself in it." Baraka, referring to Trane and others in the liner notes to *The New Wave in Jazz*, writes, "New Black Music is this: Find the self, then kill it." To pull the song is to be taken over by it.

To pull the long song, the long poem, particularly the serial poem, the extended lyric, is to be taken over and to be taken afar. *Zār* resonates with Zar, the city said to be "on the other side of far" and sometimes "just this side of far" in African American folk and literary tradition, mentioned by Zora Neale Hurston, Larry Neal, and others, including myself in *School of Udhra*, whose third and final section is entitled "Zar." Another index of *Blue Fasa's* recursive reach, *zār's* vibration with Zar continues the salience of movement, migration, transit, and nervous travel found in previous installments of *Song of the Andoumboulou* and *"Mu,"* a liminal, intersectional unrest the figure of Legba, the limping god of the crossroads in Fon-Yoruba tradition and a "transitional chord" in Harris's formulation, encapsulates toward the end of *Nod House*: "Legbaland it was and we limped on." Locality and locality's discontent continue, as do identity and identity's discontent. New names and new places appear: Mr. Pinch, Mrs. Vex, Ed, Low Forest, New Not Yet ... The place, polity and condition the poems continue to call Nub persists, having been joined, in *Nod House* (begun around the time of the U.S. invasion of Iraq), by Quag and Nod, the former its colony and itself colonized by the latter.

Nod, in *Nod House's* last passage, is said to be "Nub's / emic / retreat," *emic* being an anthropological term applied to analyses of cultural phenomena from the vantage of a participant in the culture in question, distinct from *etic*, which applies to analyses from an outsider's perspective. Nod is Nub thrown back on itself, the book's title suggesting Nub's introspection, Nub's inward retreat, a certain recoil or repercussion having to do with failed extension, *house* carrying connotations of the domestic, the private, but by way of recent parlance the public as well, Nub all the same outside or beside itself. It's an inwardness or introspection the expression "to nod off" lends a suggestion of sleep and the expression "to nod out" a suggestion of narcosis, while nod as a sign of assent, recognition, invitation, or approval is somehow part of a condition or state that aims both to be aware of itself and to be rid of itself, to extinguish and awaken itself. The title wants to carry that quandary, that qualm, as well as to imply sleepwalk. Nod is the land east of Eden, the land Cain ran away to and wandered in after killing Abel. It announces themes of exile and unrest and inner and outer extension running through the unending book.

Blue Fasa's title samples two distantly related black musical traditions, the West African griot epic *The Dausi*, which includes the story of Gassire's lute and the lost city of Wagadu, and trumpeter Kenny Dorham's hard bop classic "Blue Bossa," influenced by the emergence of Brazilian bossa nova and introduced on tenor saxophonist Joe Henderson's album *Page One* in 1963. *The Dausi* goes back centuries, sung by the Soninke-speaking griots of the ancient empire of Ghana, which arose in the fourth and fifth centuries A.D. and peaked during the tenth and eleventh. It bears upon the history of the long song, the long poem, especially the serial poem, the extended lyric, not only by being an instance of such but by virtue of Ezra Pound's recourse to its tale of Gassire's lute and the lost city of Wagadu in *The Pisan Cantos* and Robert Duncan's references to it in *Passages*, and early on arising in "Song of the Andoumboulou: 5." The repeated "Hoooh! Fasa!" in Leo Frobenius's translation refers to one of the Soninke clans, the Fasa. By the time Frobenius heard the tale sung in 1909 they and the other Soninke had long since become something of a homeless people, remnants of a once powerful empire that was eclipsed by the rise of the Mandinka in the thirteenth century, wandering with their mournful songs of the loss of Wagadu all over West Africa, throughout the Gambia, Guinea Bissau, Burkina Faso, the Ivory Coast, and other regions. The wandering "we" of this book, against the backdrop of "Nub's new entropy," come to see themselves as Fasa, by turns "truly blue Fasa" and "Truly pretend Fasa, / pretense made us blue."

Kamau Brathwaite, in his long poem *The Arrivants*, highlights a history of such intra-continental African movement, uprootedness and migration as that of the Soninke, a history of such movement by many African people, bringing it into play with the later, extra-continental uprooting known as the Middle Passage. The tale of Gassire's lute and the loss of Wagadu is one of decline and dispersal, an intra-Africa diaspora against which the out-of-Africa diaspora brought about by the slave trade resonates, just as the bloodthirsty strings of Gassire's lute are vibrated with by the African American blues tradition of dues-demanding sound (Robert Johnson, the crossroads, etc.). Both have to do with disruption and displacement, the latter in particular valorizing while evincing an absorption and a creative digestion of dislocation, the tradition of durability underscored by the *hard* in hard bop, an ability to roll with, or swing with, the unexpected and the new that we hear in the buoyancy of Dorham's "Blue Bossa." Said to have been influenced by Dorham's trip to the Rio de Janeiro Jazz Festival in 1961, the tune takes in the "new trend" or the "new wave" or the "new appeal" that was bossa nova, making what was a softening of samba more like samba, bluesier, more propulsive, more boisterous, touching it, especially during the solos, with the memory of harder diasporic times (a direction tenor saxophonist Archie Shepp takes even farther in his version of "The Girl from Ipanema"). That memory telescopes a history of creative incorporation of what was typically much more disruptive or even catastrophic, a digestion both rhythmic and "ythmic" (the anagrammatic versioning of the mythic and the clipped, syncopated form of the former coined in the course of these two series).

"Rag," from which "Rāg," phonologically and otherwise, is never that far, is both noun and verb—frayed social fabric, bareness of thread, torn cover, on the one hand, to disturb or to interrupt the rhythm or the time in a piece of music, to syncopate, on the other. The book's band of travelers, a traveling band it seems at times, avail themselves, if not as performers at least as listeners to the ever-present "box," of ragging's brief against time, the bone it picks with history and the poverty of politics, ragging rag as if to redress it, ragging rag as if to inoculate themselves. Would-be refugees from history or, as Ellington would say, tonally parallel to it, the wandering "we" of this if not every long song, this if not every long poem, especially this if not every serial poem, this extended lyric, dream and would usher in a new history. "Came together a common wish / to make real."

NATHANIEL MACKEY

I

RĀG

A NIGHT IN JAIPUR

—"mu" sixty-fifth part—

Lakshmi wept as we made our
way outward, blue devotion's
   annuity looped and led back,
reluctance's allure yet to accrue.
                            Larger
      than life, they'd lain belly to
  belly, patch of hair pressing patch
of hair, leg pressing leg, all they'd
   have otherwise been held in
  abeyance, Krishna's remnant
                        kiss…
Whatever after-the-fact embrace
  had hold of her we listened,
  bamboo hollow the heart of it,
                    bam-
  boo flute's burnt opening blown
                       on,
  hole his breath finessed… Flush
lozenge lipped, let go of. Tongue
   to've tarried on tongue less than
  a memory, sound what might've
                    been…
   Lakshmi wept as we made our
  way birth after birth, two-headed
  hollow beaten on at both ends, log
                   we
  slept in,   Mira's amanuenses,
                     mud
bouquet

      •

Sat gameless at the gaming table.
Sitar glint knuckling the night's
  one luster spoke sputter, made
  sputter speak… A diffuse kiss
                 low to

the ground, blue reconnoiter. Voice
also known as Wrack Tavern.
"Bar, be my altar," it sang...
                            Semi-
sang, semiwept, Lakshmi's bond
an abatement. Held but not had,
                            had
held, churchical girth. Caught strings
cut our thumbs... Insofar as there
was an I it wasn't hers we heard
her insinuate, of late begun to be
                            else-
where, the late one she'd one day be...
                            Semi-
sang, semiwept as we sat lost at the
gaming table, thumbs all thumbs
                            no
thumbs to hold on with... Held-not-
had was her new way, what had its
                            way
with us, held-not-had her
numb regret

                    •

Lakshmi sang as we sat stuck at
the gaming table, hands tied down
by sympathetic strings. To be
                            was
to be at her behest... Sought
                            bodily
solace, bodilessness, reluctant allure
it seemed. A certain way she
had with Krishna's going, beautiful
rebuff she made it seem... We'd
                            been
borne by a wind we hardly knew
                            was
blowing, wrung notes lingering mo-
ment to moment, phonic perfume
it seemed... Seemed it said cover,
                            seemed

it said collect, seemed it bid reaching
                              good-
  bye, went on reaching, seemed it told all
it said no… We sat aloft looking in on
     ourselves… Five layers we'd have
                              to
  get thru to get to what lay underneath.
                              A low
  hum came from under the gaming table,
  chance's debt reneged on, romance's
                              bet
called off

STICK CITY BHAJAN

—"mu" sixty-sixth part—

If I saw myself I saw myself
stagger. To see was to be in my
own way... Albeit to be went
   without looking, see caught
                  look's
  delay, see saw possible miscue,
look-see made it so... If I saw
  myself I saw myself stumble,
                saw
   myself steady myself. Quick
   step, leg stuck, saw myself
  undone. Slipped on the stairs
              I'd
  begun to go up, lay flat on the
                floor
  I'd walked across... Insofar, this
was to say, as there was an I it was
  no other, of late letting go no getting
   out. I saw myself I saw, no parallel
                track
  intruded. The voice I thought his was
   mine, no if it was me, myself my
own Mira, my own sweet Krishna,
  tongue's tip touching my ear no one's
              if not
  mine... Sufic, sulfitic, resinous, a thin
   wine tipped my tongue, took my
  feet away. Black leggings moist with
             leg-
sweat the taste of it, lost, I was no one
             else's,
  Wrack Tavern wine's bouquet unremit-
   ting, Wrack Tavern wine's bouquet
  unmerciful, lost, I was only my own, I
             lay
  flat... Less than a second I lay there. I lay
  looking up thru the ceiling. I lay looking

up at the sky. Stars were tiny pinpricks in
    the blackness the nightsky was, black
                                  leg-
    gings wafting the light they let in, Wrack
    Tavern's acrid bouquet... The voice I thought
      Mira's inhered in lifted cloth, aromatic
                                  leg-
    sweat, cloth under cloth, underness above
                                        me,
    sky-high

                •

Home's near side far behind me, took
    now a new name, I-Insofar. Voice
broke, I-Insofar resounded, ground fell
                                  away
    and lay flat at the foot of a cliff, made,
  as it slid, what I wanted moot... Voice
    broke as all escort faded, legs I took hea-
ven to be, black leggings, drummed-up
                                  equation of
    leg stride and starlight, legs' lit recompense...
      It was I-Insofar's Insofar-I, late slope
        I stood stuck on, stood if not
        stumbled, spliff-lit, metathetic
                                  remit...
    Beset by drums that were code
                          for
dreams, hair let down in the dream
    they said I dreamt, spinning wheels
        a music of sorts... Black leg-
      gings beneath her sari, said the
                                  exe-
        gete, love's understudy, he quipped,
                                  called
      himself, love's upstart, I said, instead...
So the floor fell away to my right,
north I thought, umpteenth amendment
        begun to go renegade, lacktone's
                                  chatter

the country I came to, coming-to
                              the

 glimpse I
caught

Another train pulled in as ours
pulled out. It wasn't only one
   was ours, we were in both. So
                                    we
      thought or would like to've
      thought... It wasn't so much
      they were trains as we were in
   motion, molecules, knowing or
                                    not...
   Nod's aboriginal we we some-
   times were, train window looked
out from looked into, light's worn
   promise run parallel, light's knack
                                    not
      to be caught... An empty seat sat
      beside each of us, a seat some
   ascendant one had gone up from,
      "illumined" it said in what we
                                    read
      later, "lit" the word on the street
                                    we were
      told... It wasn't music the motion we
      were in, albeit *Street Music from Outer
      Pradesh* it would've been had it been
   a disc whose notes we read. An alter-
      nate disposition it was if nothing
                                    else,
      the bone Djbai picked with Bittabai
   no longer marked us, "lit" the word
      bandied about if not "lit up," "illu-
      mined" what we took to more...

   Members, we were not to get weary,
                                    mind
   and medicine's aid at our disposal, theirs
      and any other we saw fit. It wasn't
      we were there for no reason. The
                                    seats
   of the illuminati we presumed upon
with adjacency, dared assume seats

9

beside… This wasn't one of the
trains we'd heard sung about. Music

was-

n't the motion we were in. The train, were
it a train, was an empty one, engineless,
driverless, conductorless, a small array

of

chairs beneath the blades of a slow-
moving fan. We sat around talking, non-
illuminati, two trains running arrested…

A bar-

bershop it might've
been

•

A barbershop it was and it was mov-
ing, the fan, slow-moving, a propeller
even so, molecules bruited about. Hair-
cuts were offered all of us. None

of us

wanted one but Sophia said she'd give
it a try… Itamar followed suit and
Anuncia followed, non-allegorical
hair piling up on the floor… Anuncio,

Nunca,

me, Huff, ad infinitum, each of us fol-
lowed suit… Bald as a cue ball we
each ended up. A pool hall it might've
been but remained a barbershop, long

since

no longer a train had it ever been one,
bald heads the heads of the condemned
or the contemplative, non-allegorical hair

now

allegorical, a fishbone the difference caught

in our

throats

•

No more than a moment, it immediately
passed. Again it was a train we were on,
 again we saw it was a train we were
                              on…
    Had there been music a refrain it
    would've been but it wasn't music,
    planoscape stubbly with scrub outside
      our windows, all we'd ever drawn
                                   back
    from whizzing by… We sat rubbing
 our hands, patting the heels of our hands
 together, the lit, lit-up, illumined ones
                                  no-
    ticeably absent, pilgrim outset palpably
      undone… Someone had gotten on,
    someone had gotten off, never to know
 the likes of such encounter again, never
                               hav-
    ing known before… All the same, we
    sat laughing, the barbershop's bequest.
                              Ready
 some would've said had we been asked, others
                              unready…
    Ready, unready, a tunnel
    took us
 in

An endless tunnel it seemed. So long
the time it took to go thru it our hair grew
back... It was Itamar who spoke first
as we came out the other end, "What did
                                                                that
all mean?" Sun's glare blinding almost
                                                                but not
quite, Sophia was the second to speak,
answering Itamar. "Same ol' same ol',"
                                                                she
said

•

Same though not quite the same, a
molecular moment invested us all, train
tracks loosening what we took to be
    firm earth, firm earth's fictional
                                    dis-
    patch. A lived fiction it was, no less
    real nor lamented, the philosophic
        posse we were no less insistent,
                                        no
        matter we now pulled into Outer
                                    Pradesh...
    Whereas before there'd been no
    music, absence entwined with music's
idea, here there wasn't the slightest
    idea... Anuncia looked at me and I
                                        looked
        at Huff and Huff looked at Nunca,
        philosophic posse though we were,
    sheep shorn of thought, we looked each
        at another ad infinitum... Pilgrims'
                                        dis-
may we discussed, what motion meant,
                                        why
        locality reneged... Philosophic posse
        that we were, though we were, none of
            us could say, "Not still a fool." What
    remained was to pry the one from the one,
                                            the
        two we rode concurrently from the two we
    were alternately on... What remained was
    to sort knowing from knowing, know with
                                        no
        cloud as the cloud the sun's glare created
                                        made
        the tunnel our hair had grown
        back in
glow

•

Fell back, fadeaway flesh's recon-
noiter. Came out of the tunnel as if
   we'd gone back in. Endlessly re-
   verberant echo, endlessly insinuative
                          delay…
  This the only world we'd been told but
   we'd have none of it, another we
   were also in beckoning, one we fell
                       away
from dubwise, wax what was otherwise
   bone… Legendary drop whose ar-
   rival we banged pots and pans to
                  an-
   nounce, Nub's new protuberance
   fading, fade seeming to say what soul
                     was…
   We came to a plateau that went on
   forever, flat for as far as we could
see. Itchy skin beset us, least of the woes
  we met, indigent extension, unrelieved
                   ex-
   panse… "Flat-out" was a word on
   everyone's tongue but it wasn't lan-
   guage made where we were the way
                  it
was… Some were said to be spoken to
               by the
   breakthrough snake, some to be bitten
   by the breakthrough bug. What was said
   mattered only so much, what-sayer, so-
   what-sayer so much, no way to say
                what
   was what… Flat for as far as we could
   see, so far we squinted, eyes leaned on by
                 sun-
  light, Earth a flat ball
  of dirt

Farewell said something, *metafare* some-
    thing else. I wanted to do something
that would put it all to rest, but I was only

                                        I-Insofar…

    The same went for all the others. Huff
was none other than Huff-Insofar, Anuncia

                                        none

    other than Anuncia-Insofar… Itamar likewise,
likewise Anuncio, Nunca, on and on, Sophia,

                                        on

    and on… On and on and on…
    On and

on

Stood calmly singing our demise,
Book of the Coming Flood held
chest-high, hymnal they all sang
                                    from…
   Theirs the new Night Choir, hot
   cloud lifting the ocean, low tide
   high on Lone Coast. Less alive
than when they lay dreaming, up
                                    to the
   tops of their heads in apprehension,
      knew they knew no condolence,
      knew what they knew, soon come…
                                    This
even though they were mute, spoke though
                                    their
   tongues were stuck to the backs of their
   teeth, this though ice broke without
sound… Heaven held itself aloft, fretless
      as they were fretful, regretful though
                                    it
   likewise was, yesterday's evaporative
   kiss… Lost and relived, lived and lost
      again, thus to go on until water made
      amends, the *Book of the Coming Flood*
                                    they
   sang from said… This we took in among
      shrubs, crouched behind bushes listening.
   Philosophic posse down on all fours, took
                                    it all
   in from down
low

                  •

   Close by but off to themselves,
      Nunca and Anuncio laughed, made
   light of it, "Night Choir, Shmight
      Choir, Soon-Come Choir,"
                                    her

hand roaming the small of his
back, his the ends of her hair.
  At each other as if there'd be
    no tomorrow, they the new
                              Stick-
    Rub Two, their turn, "Shmight
                              Choir,
  Soon-Come Choir" notwithstanding,
rubbed each other skinless, boneless,
    organless, gone when they were
    done, did themselves undone, nothing
      left when they were done doing...

                              Philo-
sophic posse, we paid them no mind. Night
                              Choir's
    hymn to world heat had us thinking, down
on all fours, footless. Doing it no solution,
    doing anything no solution, stick-rub

                              good

    as any but we were
    entranced

              •

Nunca and Anuncio lay to our right.
  Night Choir sang in front of us,
                              above
    us, feet barely touching the ground
they stood on, thin fingers turning
    a page of the hymnal, mouths
    elongated O's... Down on all fours,
                              footless,
  we called what we were doing danc-
    ing. We called what Nunca and
    Anuncio were doing dancing,
                              dif-
  ferent
  steps

As with the old-time people, the
word their one rescue, words
would be our rescue we'd been
tomb. Believing so braced us,
book

of the book's advantage, book of
the word's leverage, lift…
Al-

beit words were our one rescue
they were those Night Choir
sang. No way could we be free
of apprehension… But in the
state

known as fretless his and her
heads flew, Nunca and Anuncio
thumbing the book of not, not
that what would be would have to
do

with them, not that they were there
though

they were

•

    It was wasn't's grudge against
was come to haunt us, dues time
  owed eternity, time fronting time's
  decline… Night Choir caroling
                       doom,
    stoic fortitude, soon-come's
  forfeiture, default. Death omni-
vorous, life the anomaly, Night
                  Choir
  sang Saturn's rings wet, galactic
   heat the high note they struck…
Down on all fours, fretful, we
   were trying to envision what
                   was
   to come, a big wave reaching us
   inland, a big watery foot mashing us
                    flat…
We were trying to think something
   relevant, what to resort to down
on all fours, stick-rub's incan-
   descence translated, "World
               be
  with us," we begged… Down
on all fours, footless, Night Choir
  caroling the end of the world, every-
   thing heating up to be doused,
                 "World
  be with us," we begged… We
were trying to think urgency, the
   end of all things, ice melting in-
   to our living rooms, water sweeping
                 us away…
  Night Choir's crooned acceptance
   insisted it, muddied our hands
   and knees among shrubs, bushes
               we
  hid be-
hind

•

They won't soon have been
　　done with it, we thought, all
aspiration down to the taste of
　　　　　　　　　each
　　other's tongue, rub's image of
　　inwardness, losing the muse in
　　　dreams again, tremulous lip, tart
　　　　　　　　　　　mouth...
　　Was it never's announced arrival
we wondered, stick-rub's anagogic
pitch. Wasn't would never be but
　　　claim imminence, always impend,
　　　　　　　　　　it

　　seemed it said... Such it was they
lay to the right of us propounding,
Nunca and Anuncio's aposematic
address. Night Choir sounded like
　　　　　　　　steam
　　at that point, jets of steam under
　　a train. Statuesque, stern, Easter
　　　Islandish, Night Choir hissed
　　　　　　　　　it
seemed... Seem to one side, sound
　　　　　　　　　　to the
　　other, walls between which we made
　　　　　　　　　　　our

　　way

Like limbo but not as low, ludic
spell against what was to come...
  Lost habitation. Lost bodily solace...
                                    A

  new song on the box inside our
  heads blared out, an old song it
turned out to be. An old song
 sung out of context calmed us,
                            Max-

  ine on the box inside the boxes
    our heads had become, "All in
  my mind," we all inwardly
     hummed... Old souls, we
                          braced
   ourselves, Brown versus Bardo it
                              seemed...
   Seem's new sound escorted us, band
    of Insofar-I's down on all fours,
                            seem's

   new inoculative
   run

Down on all fours, footless. Thus
we came thru Night Choir's cor-
    ridor, Nunca and Anuncio no
    longer themselves, crossed
                            over
sniffing themselves... Each the
    other's inhalation, mere air,
    aroma, breath. Insisted we follow
                            suit,
    sough choir, philosophic posse's
    demur. "Premature apocalypse,"
we chided, wanting what was real,
    dream they were dreaming roughed
                            up...
    Each the other's inhumation, clutched
                            earth,
    laid body's limb-let transit, unlay's
    maculate re-
cess

MOMENT'S GNOSIS

—*"mu" sixty-ninth part*—

    Momentary release the most
they'd gotten, liberatory this
  or that debated endlessly,
philosophic posse's pet…
                    How
  to make moment more than
  moment, they kept asking,
                   how
  to make moment not elapse…
"Moment shall abide" was
  everyone's gambit, moment's
                   more
  than momentary life. "Moment's
  gnosis," everyone clamored,
"moment's gnosis," though
               mo-
    ment's gnosis meant each
    moment has its way… Thus
they'd have had it both ways,
  philosophic beginners, soon-
    come concordance ours for
                 the
  asking, the we whose adherence
                 they
    claimed… Philosophic pinch,
  philosophic phosphor… Not to
  know moment or no sooner
know than not, moment's know-
  ing nothing if not vanquishment,
               relin-
    quishment they called it instead…
  As if instead we stood around in
    circles, hunched over, heavily ex-
   haling, let go, moment more the
               less
  could be made of it, we grimaced,
  arms out, had at by bliss, misgiving,
              more

than any one feeling, flew... Fleet
release nothing if not momentary...

                                    Flew

but, fleet release,
fell back

                    •

It was gone by the time we heard
  it, galactic light's late arrival
an acoustic stand-in, light-year-like
  but shrunken, moment's remit

                                an
    odd, sonic perfume... The mo-
  ment had moved on and we with
  it, hard to know what was moment,
    what movement, knowing knowing's

                                drift
    it seemed. A dialogue between self and
  soul it came down to, link, dislodge-
    ment, time's protection, school

                                of
metamoment's arrest... Reprise contra-
  dancing demise, fallaway moment,

                                "Sky
    my rider, me on my back," each of us
  announced, a bubble in shallow water,

                                fish
talk we
talked

I was moment's novice. Bubbles
formed outside my mouth as I
  spoke, not gum though it was as
                                   if
  I chewed gum and blew bubbles,
                                        water
    bubbles as if to speak was to chew
  water… I was moment's novice, as
  were we all. I spoke on the near
side of knowing… Head filled with
                                       water,
    I talked out of my head, as did we
  all. Star-studded ceiling arched over
                                          us,
  what we made up
   kept us
awake

•

Philosophic posse's apostasy
came and went, moment's no-
vitiate no sooner begun than
                              gone.
    Less of the moment than the
moment's reflection, glimpsed
    itness the in or the of of it, we
were back to being where we
                              were…
Lapsed absence. Cosmic socket…
    Moment's token. Tantric abyss…
Refugees from all of that, we
    thought back, apostrophized
                              mo-
ment's hitch, moment's hiccup,
    "O Lapse, run abreast of us," we
rhapsodized, original sufferheads
                              one
    and all… Moment's menace ex-
    tolling the moment, all stock, all
    extension gone, time's hoard's
                              where-
abouts enticed us, an intrinsic stash
    we could almost touch… Where
was to was as was was to when, am-
    bage's temporizing scat… Of
                              the
moment beside the moment, time's
    accompaniment, off to one side,
at an angle, ongoing, this we talked
    about for days, moment's romance
                              as
    the moments went by… All talk, it
set us back, moment's gnosis more
    agnostic the longer we went on, more,
                              as we
    went on, moment's lament. Fleet release
    held us hostage albeit we went on
    and on, momentarily back at one point,

momentarily there again, all fret and

all

advance again
let go

No time soon would they've let
go, philosophic posse's prowess
notwithstanding, moment they'd've
had linger no moment, no frozen
                                    mo-
      ment, moment be as it would...
      Stared into the orange under-
      sides of their eyelids. Eyes closed,
      looked into the sun... Bubble
                              being
      bubble burst we saw we accepted,
      philosophic posse's new recruits
      more them than they were, stay's
                                    crude

      wisp un-
done

Went on about of-the-moment
    as if anything could be anything
but. Went on as if time were up
    to us… All such going on went
                            by
    the wayside for only a moment,
                                fluke
    moment we were buffeted by… It
        was a bubble we couldn't see
        outside we were in. No behind or
                                ahead,
        no there, no
    then

No time soon would they've let
go, philosophic posse's prowess
notwithstanding, moment they'd've
  had linger no moment, no frozen
                      mo-
    ment, moment be as it would...
    Stared into the orange under-
    sides of their eyelids. Eyes closed,
    looked into the sun... Bubble
                    being
    bubble burst we saw we accepted,
    philosophic posse's new recruits
    more them than they were, stay's
                    crude
    wisp undone... Null husk, no allure
to be drawn to. Rusted angel, awkward
  harp, heads thrummed... Allegoric
inklings made it seem we said more
                 than
    we said, no way, so beset by qualms,
                  could
    we say it straight... In the world again, we
    cleared our throats, coughed, kept go-
ing, abject inference behind us we hoped,
    mum the new expanse we approached.
                  Pil-
    grims' progress it might've been albeit we
    rode the Not Yet Express, pilgrims' arrest
                  we
    broke away
    from

        •

No such awakening availed... All such
advance, could it be said to've been, fell
  by the wayside. Moving was moving
on, not moving somewhere, the ostensible
                 where
    we'd arrive at forever beyond the bend,

bend we took pressed against windows
and walls and would walk, when we
                                    dis-
embarked, with a bentlegged hop... No
such when arrived, pilgrims' transit some-
    thing else than we expected, latter-day
                                    drift
    and disseisin, pilgrims' aubade and re-
    buff... Standing Rock, Moot Pass, Devil's
        Bluff loomed as ever, encumbrances we
        snuck to one side of silently, wheels almost
                                            came
    to a stop... We reminded ourselves it was a
        train we were on, outside Lisbon one mo-
        ment, outside Harare the next. Wherever
we were it was a moment we were in, apt to
                                        ig-
    nite, warrantless, without
    guarantee

                    •

    The near side of sound's end we pulled
into next. The ground exuded voices,
    choric inference underfoot, fraught
                                    choir,
    chthonic lament... Mostly we stayed
        in our seats listening. Some of us
    got up, stopped short of stepping off,
    stood listening, reluctance an allure we
                                        now
    knew for what it was, allure unavailable
        otherwise... Sound came out of the ground
but stayed close, a low-lying mist it seemed.
    Thin, synaesthetic, solemn... Nonsonance's
                                        rift
    and repair... Land's roll and run lay alge-
braic... Allegoric bone, splinter, splint...
        Sound said it all and said nothing, back
        to where it was before. Back to where we
                                        were

with a start, we heard it fade, the sound

                                                    we

  saw recede as we
pulled out

•

Long since gotten on in São Paulo,
Itamar took me aside. Missed being
    driven mad, he said, waistline, rump-
        swell, pout no longer murdered
                            him.
    Missed being murdered, he said. Late
        in the day we stood straddling the
    tracks, athwart though we rode inside...
        A new sound came up, meaningless,
                                    mourn-
    ful, lamenting meaning's end or con-
    cocting it, a story told and we were telling
        it, told and teller two and the same...
        What he wouldn't give, he said, to
                                again
    be so beset, what he wouldn't give to
    be susceptible again. Sophic chill he
    called what lay around us, the plains we
        spent millennia crossing, colloquy
                                of
    soul and self again, numb concupiscence it
        seemed... It was a lesson we turned away
                                        from
        reeling, pilgrimage's promise yet to be kept,
            null in the blink of an eye... Sophia's
                                    new
        look not unfamiliar, tugged by the earth it
            seemed. Crowfooted skin talismanic
    if there could be said to've been a talisman...
        A tossed ball's image bounding after...
                                    A
        moment ago ages between... Everything
                                        wrin-
    kled it
seemed

What he wouldn't have given, he was
    saying, not to've known it would
                        end.
  Fleet release left all else gray, water-
shed moment's moment after, a flat
  stir we stood arrested by... Sophic
                      chill
    propped us up, steeped abeyance.
  Skies we couldn't see leaned in on
    all sides, was and was-to-be together as
  one... There we stood, soul's dialogue
                    with
    self truncated, Itamar's complaint soul's
                     oblo-
    quy, sophic chill met by
    bedouin
sweat

•

It was the philosophic posse's
  tale and we were telling it, a tale
whose telling we were caught in…
    Again the gist was they were
                              going
  somewhere, the is of it arrived yet
awaited, ride said to be its own
    end but not yet, beats parsed
                            out
  on tight skin… A tolling of reeds
                          and
      high strings chimed in back of
    them. Insofar as there was a life
      they viewed it askance… There
                            was a
    life, Sophia said, thus they regarded it,
                              going's
    ghost were they to've
gotten there

STICK CITY ZAZEN

—"mu" seventy-first part—

Something Vedic on the box,
box or no box, sat ourselves
   down siphoning music.
    Place played harmonium,
                        Itamar
  gubgubi, Itamar Das he now
was… Such as it was there was
   a life, Sophia said. It seemed
   it lectured us. It sat us down…
                         Lotus-
  legged had we been looser. Stiff-
  limbed, sat even so… Bengal
it might've been, Bengal or Benares.
   It might've been Mumbai we
                       were
  in. Close but beginning to fade was
   where we were, no matter where
it was we were… Itamar's ictic sashay
  we tip-toed in on loosened our
                    backs
   as we sat… An outpost of the
  dead it might've been we were ad-
  dressed by, presences the I that
wasn't there conjured up, Itamar's
  Indic ensemble, nth phonographic
                    dis-
  patch… I pinched myself, neither
asleep nor dreaming, the I that wasn't
  there's I that was… A devotional song
the new Itamar sang serenaded Sophia,
                   wind
  bit the back of whose neck as it did
his, wind-afflicted, siphoning chagrin.
  Wan recalcitrance, not to be done
               with
grieving. Not to be enchanted, charmed…
  Songs of demise and regret were all

we heard, Itamar's Bengali lounge we
                                        sat
    entranced in, yogic had we not been
  so upset... The capoeira cliff lay be-
hind us now, another life, berimbau
    enticing the waves, bright sky, sun-
  shine's tight strings humming, sophic
                                        wicks
    words paled in whose light... It wasn't
    space we were in, it wasn't time. The
I that wasn't there's I that was wanted
                                        out,
  more than could be there we thought...
    Brazil was only a dream, likewise
India, Lone Coast amplitude a memory,
    to say there was a life part prayer...
                                        Light
    followed Itamar's lead he made it
  seem, *Live at the Make-Believe Lounge*
    it might've been, another new disc
we sat listening to, another new tune
                                        on
    the box... Iqbal we now knew his
    name was, the antiphonal way he and
he had with Sophia. There never was a
                                        life,
    Itamar said, Iqbal said. You pass on is
  what happens, Iqbal said, Itamar said,
    the way he and he had of relating, each
the other's Insofar-I bluff... What to say...
                                        What
  we said... Never was, was, we said. Was,
  never was, we said... We sat on the edge
    of no one could say what, brink we'd been
on unawares but now noticed, capoeira's
                                        Baul
  regret... Vertigo we brought from São
    Paulo, Lone Coast promise gone astray.
    As though our legs tacked eastward all
along, we sat shaking, "Bend, be our dawn,"
                                        we

entreated, stiff legs barely bent… Daybreak
brought more of the same. Insofar as
there was an I, we said, and so forth, no
matter it wasn't sophic anymore… Life no
                                        life,
we said, was never was, talked ourselves
tongueless, unable to let go of it, cross-
legged, hands on our laps notwith-
standing, sit seeking light though we did…
                                        Iqbal
we knew his new name was, Iqbal Das we
were sure. Iqbal played for the lovers we
were, sexed and cerebral, seamless, tantric
had we not been so upset… Sang insofar as
                                        we
were lovers, not all that far it seemed…
Hoarse throats attested not there yet, to
                                        say
there was a life pure
caprice

Rollaway horns were at his back
again. An invisible creek intersected the
  road he strode along, audible under
    a blanket of trees... Horns at
                              his
    back notwithstanding, he heard
  it, heard what otherwise wasn't
there. The muses' bare feet at creek's
  edge misapprehended, suspect
                                    aware-
      ness awareness even so, warning
                                woven
    into it it seemed, more than seeming,
"mu" as in mud again... So creek mud
  cooled his feet later, oozed between
                                    his
toes he dreamt. Creek mud laced with
    the horns' low lament, synaesthetic
    sludge it was... He was afraid, elated,
      again at the beginning, beginning to
                                      be
    absorbed again... Creation Rebel he'd
                                      have
      been had it been his to name himself, a
                                      long
      way around he
      went

                    •

    It was a long way around, feet shod
in cement, legs heavy. Long shadow
  trailing going out led coming back.
                              A long
    elliptical orbit, low sun... It wasn't
      there was never a life, more he'd
grown immune to it. Mud's horns
  memorial, the way no longer ahead,
                              fell

from what sky he could only guess...
Walked all the more, chatted at by
water, what was to come once recorded,
said to've been recorded, dry mud's

                             bird-

foot book... Babbled at by invisible
  water, make-believe music's pelvic
sway. There but not to be had, he thought,

                             had

at by what wasn't there... Had woken up
  from inside his mother's posthumous
apartment, next to nothing inside the kitchen

                               he

looked into, came away from grieving, sad
  albeit heavenly house... It was the long
way around he took, ushered by the drooping
lilies the horns were, Trench Town's

                         Mem-

phite run... How it might've been had it
  been his to make made him wander,

                        wide

motherly girth an idea the earth grew on...
A long way around, equatorial, rotund...

                     A

long way around it went... The horns

                       were

flowers blooming behind him, dark flowers,

                        mud

on the lip of
each bell

_____

    Insofar as there was a they the horns
answered. "By and by," the Bahamian
  whatsay went, better had he known it,
                                    "By
  and by." It was they, themselves, them,
                                  the
  mystic three or so it seemed, a dream in-
consequentializing what was to come, the
  horns' ongoing regret… A spoonful it
                               was
  or might've been, all it took, a spoonful
                               all it
  took

·

A big ellipse the big circle he came
around on, rebel he regarded himself
notwithstanding. Orbited... Fell in
               line...
  A stiff elixir, sipped only a spoon's
worth. Drooping lilies, lifted chalices
  once... We gathered creekside, greeted
               him,
    mud more than we saw, faces gone
long on shade, shallows, decoded
  the cloud he came in on... Thought
ourselves an exegete choir, dubbed
              our-
selves birds in black. Jackdaw dea-
cons we considered ourselves, jack-
daw decoding corps... Planet man we
called him, explained him to himself,
              the
  long way around he took. We were
the horns' ventriloquial extension, a
  big laugh inside our stomachs,
  emptied our stomachs, laughter let
              out
at island's edge... Sunlight coming thru
  cloud he called himself, soon-come in-
  consequence, naming come to naught,
             the
  cipher "By and by" took us to...
  "By and by," we muttered under our
breath, "By and by." Come too far to've
been there before we heard him say,
             Ba-
  equaling Jah- equaling Ra-Insofar-I's
             fetch,
we the decoding ones caught out... Came
  shoeless he said and we heard and we
  saw in retrospect mud caked his feet,
Creation Rebel all the same, cracked voice
             car-
  oling straw... Birdsong heavy inside it,

bass bamboo, eked-out hammerhead flute…
  The horns' counsel unassailable, con-
stant, bamboo though we were, low flute

                                    en-
  tablature, we the horn chorus's crest…
  All of which to say it was getting late,
   low sun scissored by tree limbs, leaves'
elocution mum. "Mu" as in mum it was,

                                  "mu"
    as in moon later, sun's low light an en-
   telechy of string, sun laid out meant "mu"
    as in moot, long since gone up, cut…
First flesh mud, sound second. Fret not,

                                  we
    said, all but sang, semisang, we the Inso-
     far-They bunch… Sound a second
body, a second chance, another time a-
  round. A long way it was and we were

                                  it,
   Creation Rebel's choric echo, escort…
He'd lain leg to leg with the undertaker's
  daughter the night before, long-legged,

                              tight-
   chested, lain all night lip to lip. Night's
   long seige came around again, creekside

                              tele-
  pathy more than
most

•

Across the way dawn's nascent grace,
morning not yet morning but "munin',"
  "'fore day" not strained enough. It was
                              "mu"
  as in mothersay, "munin'" her word,
not his. The goatfaced girl's olive smile
  no longer magnetic, "mu" as in muse
no more… So it seemed, meaning to
                              say
  so we said, we who sat unroused, un-
excited, we of the unassailable dismay…
  Anerogenous, a witnessing few it
                              was
  we were, he someone we told of as
well as one of us, blasé magus, gruff…

  We knew want's default on satiety,
fill, first light's forfeiture, day again
                              be-
  gun, day no sooner come than done
                              with,
  night's lay bounty snuffed… A banal
  circling, he complained, sun up, sun
gone, nothingness a taste toward the
  back of his tongue, banal, he insisted,
                              we
  as well… Play dead, don't be noticed,
  he said and we seconded. Inconspicuous,
we lay low… Low chorus, low-lying sky,
  Lone Coast… A night without stars it'd
                              been,
  moonless, night no light got thru… An
immunity it wanted to be. The body he
  thought was his not his, long since
                              be-
gun to go… Name not all it was, Dread
                              Choir
  though we were, dread more real than we
                              or he
  thought

What did we know and when did
we know we knew it he was asking,
  a rebellious question we thought.
                              Hos-
   tile, hopeless, loss's new recruit,
  upstart god of the ever stepped on.
Unshod. Sojourn's rut… The horns
  had gone home, we as well, unlay
                              sewn
   into the ground underfoot, stitched
                              insur-
   gency,
   scrum

ANABATIC JUKEBOX

—"mu" seventy-third part—

Skin, bone, meat, blood suspect, we
were again on our way somewhere
else. Body suspect, gone what soul
    was, Ohlone games dropping
                      painted
    sticks lay behind us, Lone Coast
    receded, we moved on... Sentient
wind we'd be one with again, lost
                  what
    soul once was. Lone Coast, honed
                  edge
we hurt our feet on, again we were begin-
ning to be gone... As though there'd
    long since been only one sun, blank
sun, the one sun sun's eventual end...
    Blank blacked in, thick indelible ink,
                      bird-
    beak stylus, again we'd soon be gone...

For now it was only a window I stood
at, a boat-bodied harp on the box as I
    looked out. Mamane looked over my
shoulder, "Reverend King" the next
                  cut
came up... Laughter broke out, we'd
    all been weeping. Sob held at bay by
    giggle, we burst out laughing, happy
                to
hear time turn back... Trane's bass reed
    made us laugh, keep crying, Dolphy's
    clarinet's high carouse... Ribcage theater.
    Tease. Tickle. Long fingers working
                  what
    was down   deeper, laugh though we
did although we wept. We slapped hands and
    were laughing, happy to be young again,
                    glad
    not knowing better,
    knew better

•

Not one death but many we'd heard
and of breath now said the same, the
other box the box we were stuck in,
  sound our one release. Bent pitch

                           gave

  rise, we insisted, to what words gave
    reason to be, each the eventual
    ghost we sometimes were, each
that all would end up there… An

                         an-

  nouncement, notes posted as we
  made our way out. One felt a
    friend's gaze cross one's
right shoulder, what one looked

                           at

    also looked at from in back…

  Husk it was one heard, its unsteadi-
ness. Reed's unwieldiness the boon
it now was, captious, we heard it crack.
    Thus the birdboy's dreamt kin

                         came to

  include us, cracked husks' fissures
    whispering, droll whistle we fell
    back from… A Sahelian furtherance
it was we heard, Salif Keita, another

                           new

    cut on the box. We pursed our lips,
    bit seeds albeit the box fell apart, the
      utopic box it continued to be…
    Pursed our lips, bit seeds, gap all

                           that

was left, bit seeds broke our teeth. Air

                           sucked

    in thru the all the emptiness was, bodiless,

                             we

  all stood as
one

Sprung polity's pneumatic jukebox
it was my friend and I surmised, each
   of them the ghost he or she would
   eventually be, crevice and protuberance
                                    moot...
   What would be there... What would
   not... Friend whispering into one's
   ear maybe not, polity we stood as
                              though
   we were... The window showed a shoe-
box garden, green's wild edge turned
   in on green itself, blade rolled into each
                                    leaf,

   blood each leaf's
reglet

•

We stood transfixed by the box's
pull upward, a balloon or a kite it
  might've been. A new cut sang
the singer's beloved, recalled her
                                dressed
    in only a scarf and on the scarf
   the smell of neck sweat, late night's
     agitant perfume… It was the
  glass's way of speaking we
                              saw,
   windowpane bell jar thick…
Worried would we get there,
 what we saw be what we'd
                            get,
   belled horns bellow again…
 "Reverend King" came back
    to us, neck sweat notwith-
    standing, belled horns' bellow,
                              bray…
  We stood reminded we'd been there
                              before,
    caught in the walls' rumble,
   saltbox dismay we swayed
inside

　　　　　　•

　　Rumble was back, rubble, wall all
　window again... Atlantis. East St.
　Louis. Either. Might've been
　　　　　　　　　　both...
　　It was a march we were caught
　up in, commencement, a march
　we consoled ourselves. Marched
　albeit we stood unmoving, stood
　　　　　　　　　　　hoisted
　　high we'd have said... Jericho
　we'd have said, wall falling, wall
　　all rung even so. Hoisted, al-
　beit we stood our legs dangled,
　　　　　　　　　　feet
　　came off the floor... The horns
　played hurt it sounded like. We
　ascended the wall that wasn't
　　　　　　　　　　there.
　　Where were we we were gone
　so soon we demanded they tell
　　　　　　　　　　us,
　　see-thru brink an abeyance, my
　friend and I and the we I what-
　　　said... We were spawn of
　　what tore loose, our legs
　　　　　　　　　dan-
　　gled, mud clumps fell from
　　our feet. A call climbed our
　throats as though it were we
　　　　　　　　　the
　　horns enlisted, "mu" what
　　was otherwise wallstuff, adobe,
　　　　　　　　　col-
　loquy of
　straw

•

   "Abide, my friend," I heard myself
say, the box's mouthpiece it seemed.
  Wood lips, box head, box body. "Abide,"
    I said even so… It wasn't Huff,
                         how-
    ever much it seemed so, the friend
    who stood at my back and to my
    right. Box head, wood lips, box
                       body…
  Shadow box. Cardboard insides…
  "Abide," I said, more to myself it
might've been, wood lips, box body,
                    box
    tongue… Late aspect. Late luxurious
                      music…

   Endless till it ended
  we found
out

Stood happy-sad at the sonic window,
Om mani padme hum the glass we
looked in thru, bell as in bellow
                              again…
  "Fret not thyself," my friend said
it seemed I said. Bell as in bellow
blared on… Death-obsessed friend
and foe, witch's familiar, "Fret
                              not
  thyself," I did say… Empty window,
                              "mu"
  as in moot. "I do believe," I said it
  seemed I
said

BEGINNING "WE THE MIGRATING THEY"

—andoumboulouous étude—

We the migrating they we
instigated, those in whose
name we went. To get where
   they were going and lie
                     down
was all we wanted, love's
   choric voices convening,
caroling home, home ex-
   ploded long since… It was
     up and be gone again,
                       crab
   shell taken for sun where
there was no sun, without
   or about hope no one could
                   say…
   We the migrating they we
stared out at, prodigal wish to
burn elsewhere intransigent,
   Stella's high skylight were
                  Stella
   suddenly one of us, she the
   one who said move on…
     They were not the dead
                 but
dolls of the dead, a dream of
   coming back as we were going.
Eyes wide but eyes nothing
              looked
   out from, effigies adrift in the
                  dark…
   A parsed pomp and circumstance
it was, not being there but the
   image of being there what they
were caught in, lagleg retreat,
               emic
   advance… Inside the bubble
the house became we saw each
   awake one, puffed-up

ascendance all there was of
com-
ing back, an effigy of each if
not
each its own effigy, each an un-
likely remit... Everyone someone
we
knew, resemblance mocked us,
faces doll hard, clavicles crossed.
Each with a big mouth, telling on
everyone, what so-and-so did,
what
so-and-so thought... Who they
otherwise were we fell away from,
equate their going with our going
though we did... Who they were
they
otherwise were, the away what there
was
of it still

We the migrating they they
said come see, lean though
we did and look, sort of see,
    night sky no less remote.
                        They
    were the stars, we the stars'
        understudies, night's
love love's lit recompense,
    night's far fetch a black
                        well
    dipped into, horns' bells
        burrowing in... Would-
be recompense. Ythmic
largesse... Far fling as if all
    touched other, we their
                        press
    outward unimpelled...
                        They
    the open sea and we the raft
I clung to, left leg scissored
    by hers, we lay ensconced,
                        we
    within the we they elicited,
        ours newly raveling out...
Not to be attached we told our-
    selves, ratchetless advance
                        we'd
    come abreast of lip to inquis-
        itive lip, tongue to ingenuous
    tongue... Lift it otherwise was
                        no
matter, we drew back, we's rum-
    maging they let go. An exercise
in touch it turned out to be, we
    their would-be stand-in, pre-,
                        post-,
    pan-pronominal consort, to see
ourselves we set ourselves adrift...
    Curve and declivity. Protuberant
                        hip...

Immanent ether. Astral dispatch…
They light's arrival's delay, we
their someday stand-in, ages we
                                    took
    to reach them, we the migrating
                                    they…
    That they were roots in the sky
    moving's muse insisted… Star flux…
                                    Far

star… Far fix

We the migrating they their
   studies in touch. Stand to
their step, a studied pass, we
   stood… Studies inasmuch
                           as
   we were steps, we stood.
   Studies, we ran in place…
   Stood what they'd have called
                        pat,
   we called ready, poised on a
     brink we saw fall back…
   Stood, we wanted to say,
                    what
chance there was were chance
   in doubt, step stand's re-
   condite flicker, step stand's
                  tonic
   duress… "Blue Bossa" came
in from a distance, a version no
   one had yet heard. Step some
    indigenous drift it turned
   out, led to export stay, Stella's
                 man-
   date notwithstanding, end wanting
    what would not be there… It
   wasn't music but a stepped ab-
scondity, a music before music's
                 com-
   promise. Stand resisted step, step
  stand, moot martyrdom, stride's
   true marriage's bossa, Itamar
                 and
Stella's vow… A stepped incon-
    sequence it might've been,
   automatic étude, step's new
   nonchalance. They the migrat-
  ing they the step we took, step
                 the
stand we took… Step, we wanted
                 to

say, stood in stay's way. It was
the old and new school we were
enrolled in, syllabic devotion
recalling Baul, Bengali, qawwal...
                                        Scat
academy grads though we were, we
bit our tongues, beat back say's ex-
cess. They the migrating we were
automatic, step's expected star
                                        so
imminent a winding stairway it was
we were on... School of tangency,
glancing contact... Blasé stasis...
                                        Pre-
tend impasse... Never not to've gone
but be going, a stepped incumbency...
Step's evacuated finality. Finality's
                                        evac-
uated fit

We the migrating they trans-
lated. Draft meant drift meant
scheme meant sketch. We
                    the
    migrating they were back
in school… Step's incline
    toward stride, we stood in-
structed, theirs the advance
                    we
    were learning, rote's auto-
    mata, rail we were bound by
scraped as we verged outward,
                    we
    the magnetic they they turned
    out to be… Step fell away
the longer we lasted, collapsed or
    contrived itself anew. There
                    was
    a rail one stood at, stuck where
    one stood, caught by Stella's
backsides the way she went
    forward, celestial mechanics,
                    cos-
    mic rump… Itamar called it
    astral, heavenly. Chant the names
    of God we were told… Ita-
mar. Stella. Scrape, caress,
                    ca-
    reen… Crab, sun, bell ad
infinitum… A worked incerti-
    tude it seemed albeit abounding,
insist, "I do believe," though
                    we
    did. Scrape, caress, careen,
    crab, sun were all names.
    Bell another name, they went
on and on… Stride, bubble,
                    rum-
    mage a rut we were caught
in, ran only running in place.

Rotating stations we worked
                              our
    way loose from, effigy, skylight,
                                  scat...
    Ran as though pedaling, knees at
        one's chin. Curve, doll, declivity.
    Lip, leg, star. Name after name
sang change, rang changes, God's
                                need
    not to be still... String the names
        as one we were told, one with-
out need of us though they were,
                                  we
        the migrating they again going,
        raft, root, tangency, touch... A
studied sputter, spin, step taken
                                up...
    Ratcheted, not yet ratchetless. Fix,
                                    dip,

        flicker. Brink, stair-
    way, step

DOOR PEEP SHALL NOT ENTER

—"mu" seventy-fifth part—

A glimpse of what otherwise
went by unseen. Quick stir we
   were told was what soul was,
   bedouin flashback, furtive tab-
      leau… Saw their tongues
                                    lift
away, let loose, dark's dilated
   aperture flex his jaw. Damned
her hard head, she said, no matter
                                    it was

   his were it hers to complain…
   Hiked rumps clouded it, she'd
      have said. An odor of incense
made its way out we knew was
                                    ner-

   oli. On edge, we were cracks
in the glass we looked in thru,
      heard and sensed we saw what
she'd have said were her way to
                                    com-

   plain, complaint a condition of
      soul we could see… Heard and
   sensed we saw what she'd have
                                    said

   or said she'd have said. No way
not to, we said… Seesay had its
   way with us, no matter we resist-
      ed. Cracks in the glass cut their
                                    lips

as they put their lips against the
   glass we looked in thru… They
the andoumboulouous two again,
                                    the

   he and she whose legendary
travail we saluted, stood looking
      out and drew back, bore wit-
ness, they the witnessing two we

saw… Winged ember the he-say

      she-

say, anger's rendezvous with
 incense pendant, neroli's cheek
underness rotund… Low-lying
 perfume, splay funk, fey tactility…

       Es-

sence reached at raged over, stiff
intangible, stuck-sun aroma they
 could touch. Smoked intangible,
each the other's no mo', each

      the

other's used-to-be twin… To
want to've been otherwise, what
 not be what, operatic itch and

      ip-

seity, soon-to've-been-gone's
dread nuff… Cracked window,
 cracked wall, rickety testament.
 Dread nuff no more than a

     whiff,

nothing we saw. Nothing we
 heard held sway… Nothing so
true as the smoke in our noses,

      burn

and extinguish-
ment's musk

When it was we I saw I saw
myself revive. Proverbial water
 woke me, abstract, dry. Thus
 the one thing that we all thought,

                                   up
   I sprang as though flung…
   Yonder's far wall then, wail
 though we might, a book whose
   one page we thumbed. It

                            was
the book of not getting there
   yet, wake though I did and
 spring, lunge forward. All

                         that
   lay fallow drew me on, dread

                            nuff's
   bond and
 rebuff

Up the hill and on the other
side saw them, inside whose
  heads tape wound and re-
    wound, acoustic bandages,
  wound heads humming,
                      spun…
Slapped Calabash the name
  their condition went by,
  name not taken lightly we
now saw. Whirling earth
                took
  their legs out from under
  them, theirs the upset ipseity
                   we
  met… Reminiscing the fog
  on Lone Coast, we inched
our way down. We saw it
  sit there, strict incumbency
                we
  scratched at hoping to up-
  root… Not to be budged, it
    sat, Squat Calabash. Slip
              to
  sit's recalcitrance, we inched
                our
way across… Slid where the
  ground went gravelly, barely
  out from the foot of the hill
we'd been on. Saw them, we
                the
  ones they'd heard were com-
    ing, long-lost calabash kin
they got wind of, soon-come
    could we catch up… It was
                ours
  to advance, their wound heads
  exhorted, hummed ahead of
us, might've been bees. Soon's
                high

              hope stayed abreast of them,
          theirs to hold out as we trudged
            on… Heart's hope, atavistic
                              wish…
What the dead died wanting pro-
          pelled us, made us weep, not
        to go likewise, not to abide,
            trudge though it was, all it
                              was…
          We the migrating they again,
        scrounge though we did, run
            low, wear thin, theirs the new
                              day
          not come… History was time's
        affliction, eternity's compromise…
                              Came
          to meadow's edge massed as
          one, gravelliness gone, sat sipping
                              pi-
        geon
broth

The marine layer lay behind
us, we'd gotten ahead of our-
selves. We were doing what
   we could, whatever we
                    could,
did what we could to be
   there... Pebbles notwith-
   standing, we were there,
                    we
told ourselves, tack though
   we did, no matter telling's
detour, doing what we could
                    to
   be there... How could we
not was the calabash academy's
   question, how be anywhere
but there. No amount of pigeon
                    broth
   set us at ease though we said
   amen, how not and how be
                    any-
   where but
there

•

Abstract alterity sophic chill's
far side. Pebbliness we slipped
  on, slid. By night beset by doubt,
    by day crept onward. "Back
                        when
  I believed I'd live forever," some-
    one had been saying before
  the connection broke... A match,
it sounded like, had been struck
                          and
    went on being struck. Endless
  ignition, it sounded like, it went
    on, unending... Static. Rasp and
                        abra-
sion. Scuff... Revelatory burr-head
    hindrance, revelatory burr-head
    spur... Beyond the next hill a meadow
      waited we'd been told. Revelatory
                          burr-
    head brush... The head of an ax in a
  bowl of river water. The stars or the
      moon reflected in a well. Some-
where these had meaning we'd read...
                          So
    it went or so it was we went on think-
ing. Scrub, uncultivability otherwise...
    Soon-come inconsequence, next to
                        no
    end. Unstrung lute, moot calabash.
    Resonance's end could there've
  been one, nonsonance's day thus
                      be-
gun

It was something Ed might've
said, Ed Itamar's new moniker.
A bit of whatsay hung in the
                              air.
What the dead died wanting
echoed again… "When your
people begin to go," Ed said,
  leaned with his arm around
                              Stella.
Waved goodbye looking over
                              their
  shoulders, torn sleeves caught
in the wind… Where they stood,
could stand be said to be what
they did, stayed indefinite,
    strayed, where what they
                              did
  do stood, we as well… All
address, all advance, all re-
    cognizance all at once faded,
fell into idle chat, small chatter,
                              point,
  had we had it,
let go

We pounded the heels of
our hands together gently.
  What to say, what to say,
                        what
    to make of it... It was they
    were the awaited ones or
  we were the awaited ones, not
impossibly both... Calabash
                        kin,
    we accepted. The call came
    thru, collect, it went without
      saying... Clung to what we
                        could,
    clung to what came loose.
    Raveling... Unraveling...
Clutched

For spirits, ambivalence and ambiguity are windows of opportunity.... *Zār* is a kind of metalanguage ... an ingenious comment on the existence of ambiguity in human affairs.

—Janice Boddy, *Wombs and Alien Spirits: Women, Men, and the Zār Cult in Northern Sudan*

HOFRIYATI HEAD OPENING

—"mu" seventy-seventh part—

Pigeon broth carried us over,
        spilled over, spoons above
    our heads as we descended.
                                        Zar
        the city we came to, *zār*
    one's host and rider, northern
    Sudan arrayed at one's feet...
    Spoon our bane and balm,

                                        we
    cried, "Spoonful," red wind
        in from the east. "Spoonful,"
    I crooned and cried, "Spoonful,"
                                        lo-
    quats inside my head outside my
    window, bunched-fruit umbilicus
    held at bay... Loquat cluster con-
        noted youth, I fell back singing,
        voice giving out as I got to my
                                        fa-
    vorite part. Song of the otherwise
        unsung it turned out to be, loquat-
    connoted lapse... I was the lady
        among the leaves and I was the
                                        lord
        looking up from under, our legs'
        open book's interpreter... I wore
    red, I wore wide-legged pants and

a billowing shirt… I wore a shawl,
                                        I
   wore a fez, a jalabiya… "Spoon-
ful," we crooned again, wooed our
   host and rider, lady of the loquat
clump we rode and were, thread's
                                        tight
   wind and release… We of the big
seed, we of the blunt cluster, an
   old illness older than books. An
                                        an-
cient updraft, we wanted waftedness,
                                        whiff,
   incense banishing
sweat

                •

   Head split, burgeoning seed it
      seemed. Ax's edge and head my
   headdress. Respiteless, Hofriyati
                                        stress…
   Parallax made me sick. Parodic
husband. Parodic wife. Parodic ram's
   head smeared with henna, *zār* was
                                        my
   prince, my pride… Lit sticks lay
on the floor between my feet, floated
   incense. Thread was the pull of
      the air… Attitude, moment
                                        of truth…
   Lurch… Parallactic dispatch…

   We were what we wore. What we
   wore became us. Drums led, strung
   us along, beats quick stitches.
                                        Thread
   connected us, we wore pants, we
wore skirts. Thread costumed us,
   held us up, made us up, branch
                                        bent

by his and her wind affliction…
                                    Illness
older than books its own book, book
of what was barely there. Sewn lips
no impediment, drumspun, dreamt
                                    we

possessed
ourselves

There were notes hung from
branches, faint, scribbly what-
    nots, sound more than scent,
  Lebanese perfume. We splashed
                                    it

    on, parodic excess, winced,
    wandered off... So much for
      turned heads, we said, say-it-
  again's envoys. So much for
                                turned
    heads, we said...   Heuristic
    Egyptians, we ate chickpeas,
  hawks' heads, Horuses, washed
                                    it
    down with pigeon broth, sat,
                                sipped,
      shook

●

"Spoonful," I sang out, "Spoonful."
    I was possessed. I wasn't there. I was
a woman, a man, one or the other,
    sometimes both. Spoonful my
                                pledge
    and protest, I sang it soprano, I
    sang it baritone… They pulled a
twig from under my skin, boiled it
    with onions, called it soup, spoonful,
                                heart's
    content… I stood on stilts, it seemed I
saw England. I saw frenzy all around,
    I wasn't there… I wore thread. Thread
                                led
me on, I stood on stilts. It seemed I saw
    Babylon… Thread's far side, cloth
    covered me, there though I wasn't
                                there.
    Spoonful filled me with distance,
    eminence, ghost what I was, guest
I'd have been, Zar's new inhabitant, me…
    Thread led me on, fed me, twig taken
                                out of
    my chest a new suit, spoonful's gruel
    my regret. "Spoonful," I groaned,
    again "Spoonful," spoon so abrupt it
                                broke
thru… Spoon my disguise, my redoubt, I
    was obsessed. Thread my dismay, I was
                                up-
set… Spoon hit the side of my head, set
    me off, dystrophy's dance I knew… Al-
legoric spill, allegoric sprawl. Allegory
    meant someone was watching…
                                "Spoon,"
I said and said again, sighed more than
    said. Spoon's alibi thread cut my
    lip, I lay entranced. Spoon dug inside
my skull, scooped out what was there…
                                Spoon

lifted me up, let me down, I looked over

my

shoulder... Filled me. Foreboding...
Fret

A cracked head's hymnal sung
from. So it seemed as we and I
came down again. On the banks
                              of the
indifferent river recollected loquat's
low-squat ruse. Made our way
                              to-
ward Medicineville, getting
better, balm the hasp hair was,
                              lock
where legs
met

II

RAG

Halloween candy on their
lips as their lips met,
he and she whose thrown
                        hips
    he'd been hit by, rump
    truncheon, runaway motif
    zār made its home in,
rag auspice it would come
                        to
    be called... *Zār* set them
    down before a threadbare
strand of earth, Globe Coast,
    allegorized ocular prosthesis,
                        glass
    eye they wiped clean with
    a tattered cloth... Come to
this, two Andoumboulou cajoling
                        a
    rusted sun, spawn of such con-
    geries none could be more
conjoint, each be as they were
                        be-
    fore, each be gold again,
    beside themselves astride each
    other, each be burst again...
Woke from a dream the world
                        had
    been taken away, woke to
    find it had, his were it hers
    to claim, hers were it his,
theirs not to belong to again.
                        Them
    against the world, what of it
    was left, them against what
    was there... Held each other,
they the sincere ones, held each
                        other,
    shook, let go. Intimate lip, neck,
    shoulder blade, rough below

the waist, quick riches not to
                          be
   kept… But the halloween
candy stuck. This, they thought,
   would maybe mean forever.
As close as ninety-nine to a
                          hun-
dred they'd be, the battle for
   the house outside the house
   no less near, Knot neither
                          Not
nor Nod House, debris outside
                          the
      bed kept
      at bay

                  •

   Suspect ipseity, ipseic
hide and seek, rummaging
   a suspect heaven. An
abrupt unremittingness
                          of
pine, blue forest, locked
   inside her mind's dilated
   eye… A long way from
                          Lone
Coast, a new or another
   world, a window it might've
been she looked in from…
      Immortal for a time,
      laughed accordingly, she
                          of
the large mouth, she of the
                          knotted
   cloth, Our Lady of the Nylon
Run… Our Lady of the Teeth
   and Gums by his rendering,
                          she
      of the horse laugh he loved…
      A trumpet's blown leaves

fell past the window loss lay
                    be-
  yond… All to no end but
    absolution. All to no end
                              at
all

_____

Elegiac repose time cut
its teeth on, all at Mr. Pinch's
expense. Mr. P sat silent,
                                       brood-
    ing, P for possession, P as
in leapt, leaves coming
    down his dismay, mock
squander, foliage's mulch
        cascade... Sat now at
                                       in-
    sufficiency's table, the
    one, the one-half, that
won't do. Antiphonal
thread hung from his cuff
                                       un-
    raveling, a bit of thread's
                                       inex-
    tricable
    stitch

　　　　　•

　　Mr. P meant she pinched
herself, unsure she was awake.
　Felt it. Winced even. Was.
　　Costume courtesy had
　　　　　　　　them
　　in its thrall, she and Mr.
　P, costume thread they hung
　　by… We the witnessing
chorus knew Mr. P as well,
　　　　　　　　pinched
　　ourselves. Autumn's leaf
　costume had us dreaming,
　　no way to wake up, costume-
courteous escapade… They
　　crunched Halloween candy,
　　　　　　　　hard
　　candy, before they kissed, cos-
tume-courteous regress. *Zār*
　　was the lozenge they sucked,
　　　　　　　　bit
　　down on, Zar the far country,
high cry they came down from,
　threadless before they came down…

　　A serenade they were elected by,
sound their recompense, costume-
　　courteous rhapsody, thread they
　　　　　　　　were
　　accosted by… So that what we sang
　　was less itself than what we heard
them say they saw, we their antiphonal
　　　　　　　　alibi,
　　we the awaited
ones

•

Now they were older, Hal-
loween candy Halloween
    candy. Saw thru the
    wishfulness of it, rags
        they were in underneath…
                                Sag's
        rough cloth a new ultimacy
of cloth, old and new naked-
    ness nearness's forfeit,
late anerogenous collapse…
Napped inwardness inside
                                out
    it seemed it was, beast out
at beauty's behest but free
    of it, slack skin ominous
                                in-
stead… The earth an arm
    tugging them, gravity's
    caress, gravity's decree the raw
        coat they were caught in,
                                thread
    they were pulled on by. They
the new landscape, lonescape,
    this their new condition, Globe
Coast… Thread the earth hung
                                by
        theirs again, beginning to
    be gone but glowing, blue
    rotundity, fadeaway gleam,
then gone. Planet Zar it might
                                've
    been, so distant it made them
        weep. "Beautiful," they'd
    said as it receded, took it back
                                now,
    knottedness thread's new de-
gree… A new tense they will
    have coined it said, quipu-like,
the new time still to come.
                                New

night, new day, telescopic, it
                              said,
    soon to have been come to,
sooner come undone, soon's
    new summit come down from
    belatedly, soon they say was
                              there
    not come… Halloween candy
no lozenge, they the quote-unquote
    cosmic two. They the divine
      game they made of it, his to
      be hers to be mobius, thread
                              res-
    plendent, looped… Came into
    post-allegoric remanence,
they the planetary two. Inland
                              reach
      beyond the Bay of Said they
    came to, came to quote-unquote
                              where
    thread ran
    out

         —————————————

"Please, please, Mr. Pinch,"
we heard them say. No more
  testing was what they wanted,
                       no
    more not knowing. Wanted
  that where they were be where
    they were, wanted that they
                     not
be so unsure… As did we, who
  were wind inside the walls,
and we repeated them, "Please,
                 Mr.
  P, no more names. Will there
ever be no Knot, no Nod, no
    Knock House, when will it be
                   home
  again"

       Wet their fingertips,
tested the wind. Hurried
  breath inside the wall
                        had
    them teetering. Took
what they took to be
  flow a step further,
                    heads
above their heads lifting
  higher, hot sky, sucked
air brimmed with light…
    Barefoot imperium,
                        un-
  shod epiphany. Unsprung
apocalypse remanent. Holi-
  day's unkept promise
  unlamented, up thru it all
                        they
went… They saw the other
  side coming down, pale
  reach otherwise withdrawn,
                        re-
luctant, slipped out for lever-
  age, caught… Beauty
  bought dearly they thought,
                        late
  thought, lost as they ascended,
let go… Mr. and Mrs. Pinch,
 P for short. Each the other's
made-up half the myth went,
  halfway had them ravenous,
                        on at
    in-between's behest. Whole
might half suffice, knew better,
    remote philosophic sun…
    Remote feeling they had
                        the
  whole was not the half of it.
Wondered was what there
                        was

all there
was

•

A large garment floating
down with stars under it,
  batted about by wind in
waltz time. They'd gotten
                          up
  from insufficiency's
  table, sort of a séance,
ice-rink bossa nova no
  more... Night's gown
  studded with stars,
                      ec-
clesiastic, tugged hem
  ripped as they groped
  upward,   heaven's
                      half-
way dispatch. A halfway
  house of sorts, a sort of
  alembic, buffeted one
  way and another, to
                    and fro...
  Make-believe band whose
  no-notes they intuited,
the Overghost Ourkestra
  blared in the background,
                        loose
  gown's ripped equivalent,
empty seams' exhalation of
  air... Threads of eyelight let
                            them
  dangle, somewhere looking
  led them to... Canopic strain,
canopic viscera... What was
                          what
  would not
do

ANACOLUTHIC LIGHT

—"mu" seventy-ninth part—

Sat exchanging notes on what
  was to come, not knowing
what, so obtuse an adumbration
  of light we were ecstatic,
                      no
  matter we were in tatters, tossed...
  Even so, we went on as if,
an if that in the end became
  incipient, beginning to come
                    on
  so recessed we were taken
aback, unaware we could be
  so unaware but knowing
                  it
now, endlessly agnostic regret...
  What were we talking about
the what-sayer came to life
    again to ask us. Tempted to
  answer damned if we knew,
                we
  stood and took it, steeped our
intended book... "Light let
  us down," we said at last,
                ad
hoc epiphany. The what of it
  silhouetted, we were elated
all the same, sat sensing we
  were protected, tarp tatter,
              in-
terstice, canopic stir... Light
undulant, light corpuscular,
  light's coincidence occult...
             So
  it was we wore not knowing
lightly, made light of it. "Light
  let us down," we said again...
  Heads held high even so, arms
              lifted,

praise lay unassuming otherwise.
An oblique noise if not noise's

                                hem-

  orrhage. Light's fey cartilage
  blocked, blue fidget, filigree's

                                    filigree,

fuss… I would have none of it…
I drew back in newly gnostic re-
  gret, relived my awakening.
The Overghost Ourkestra Live

                             at

  the Lighthouse could not have
    sounded a more distraught
note… That there'd be no
  between seemed likely, so

                           close

  we'd have been, so close
had I not drawn back but I'd
  have none of it, drew back,

                          what-

  sayer inside… So went the
life I elected, parallax antinomy

                       not

  to know stillness, whatever we'd

                         have

said I'd have
said no

●

It might've been Stick City we
were in, each word a baton we
could barely get a hand on, a
                              stick
so animate nothing stayed put,
each word pulled away, walked…
Made-up outcrop the auspice
of the eye approximated, a world
                                 we
stopped and stood and looked
    at, distant, resplendent, raw…
Made up for lost outwardness,
                                the
retreat Stick City was, bodies'
    rebuff the we I drew back from,
rebuff the sound of crickets in
    the end. Outpost of soul we
    expected foreclosed on, body
                              just
enough to abide light's modest
    body, body just enough to get
                              by…
    It was light's dilated cry and then
    it wasn't, light's own Eleven Light
    City, no sooner come to than
gone. An insurrectionary swarm,
                              light's
own Elysium, sound more than sight
    even so. So we sat, trading notes
    adumbrating light's eventual ambit,
                                   sat
breathing in, breathing out… Cloth
fell away from our shoulders. Now
    no more than thread was left.
                         Light's
modest body it was we now said yes
    to, skin broke thru like bone…
    Cloth fell away from our backs
    as we stood up, rags draped our
                              feet

if we walked. Pharaoh's trunk it was
   we wore, sonic swaddling, light's
                                    mod-
   est body, sound... I sat on a bank,
      a boy again, overlooking a stream.
What, what, what, what, what was
   all I knew to say, what, what, what,
                                       what,
      what... Had we been a band a neo-
   platonic band we'd have been. A
      philosophic sound ensemble, we
dealt in light, light's audiotactile
                                    equi-
      valent, rough equivalence, rough
      cloth covered us again... We were
   not a band, all we did was listen,
                                    sit
sipping herb... Chopped capsicum,
      winced as we remembered, lost
   in eye squint. "Chalice be our
      witness," we thought, thought's
                                    abra-
      cadabra. "Chalice be with us,"
                                    we
   thought

I fell into dreamless Atlantean
   sleep, no wish to fulfill, Mr.
and Mrs. P's apprentice. The
                             we
   I fell in with grew larger than
any other, calabash, capsicum
   and chalice each only a thing,
    nowhere if not Stick City's
                           far
  side, smack-dab on its out-
 skirts I knew… I sat brookside,
   squatted, knees against my
                       chest…

  Fleet prelapsarian
vignette

Touched but unable to seize
it, I saw light. The old books
were back again… Or they
                        were
    the new books but I was
old and saw nothing new,
    so resigned I saw looking,
                        not
    light

Mr. P sat humming inside
a house overlooking the sea,
  cracks in the window, a
  draft in the room... It was
                  some-
  thing for the dead the dead
  might have said, the dead
   said to be dying of thirst...
Something blew in, something
                    blew
  thru. Mr. P prestidigitated,
  hummed... It was Dogon 101,
   we were there again. Pinch
come to shout, we were there...
                 Same
  note, new octave, there again...
Lone Coast seacliff the reach
  of Bandiagara, P the prestidigi-
tator hummed... I fell away, Mr.
                  P's
  apprentice. Mr. P was Mr.
   Press I thought. It was either
  hedge or be caught out or even
                 both
  it was intimated... Thus it was that
  I'd have come there, powderkeg
planet, year sixty-four since my
               arrival,
  two eights met and multiplied...
  It was one, it was the other. It
  was neither, it was both. All
                 I
could say was it was... I heard
  waves. I heard a symphony,
  strings welling up the swell of
              salt
  off Lone Coast. Lone Coast no
             coast,
  no way to say it
was

•

Mr. P corrected me… No coast
not so much as no known coast,
    lone and *no known* were in it
together. Golemlike, *lone* and
                              no
    known walked hand in hand.
So spoke Mr. P… "Please,
    please, Mr. P," we begged,
                         "don't
say that. *Lone* would never be *no*
    known's kith and consort, *lone*
    would never be that way." Silly,
but so it went, pilgrim's progress
                              no
    progress, nothing to go on about…

    Otherwise it was all copacetic.
    We had some chaabi on the box
                              and
we were moving, a trek we could've
    sworn we coaxed music from, culled
                              what
    condolence
we could

Dirt slid from cliffs as we
drove up the coast. It was real,
  neither not nor not known
                          but
      escorting us, Highway
  101 where it ran with 1,
    Pismo Beach, chaabi on
  the box the next world we
                          were
    almost in, Algiers it might've
                          been
we were in... So real we wept,
    remembering. Resemblance
  did us in... I wrote a letter
                      to
    myself remanding the hand
  of Mr. P, my head inside his
    head inside my head correcting
his, him inside mine correcting
  me... Mr. P was Mr. Past, I
                      was
    raiding the present... Silly that
                          it
    came to
that

·

Mr. P was the outermost
me, I wanted to say, the in-
ner me's mime and remit
I made it seem, soon-
come key to the highway,
                          iden-

tity's ruse and regret... I
was beginning to be less
attached I thought. I wrung
my hands inside the car,
wanted out, we were welded
                          in,

Anuncia riding shotgun,
feet propped on the dash-
board, everyone we knew
bunched up in back... Soft
Anuncia's hard feet led
                          the

way, we were heading
north. Nothing if not
love's high cry transported
us, love's high cry, love's
                          col-

lapse... Recalled when the
underside's rise meant
something sexual, now not
                          that

but catastrophe, death. No
coast if never to see Lone
Coast again, Shell Beach
lay to our left. A low tolling lay
left as well, bell, buoy. Low
                          groan...

Omen... Gruff... Not yet
there no matter where we were,
we of the phonographic
diaspora motored on, we of
                          the

inconsequent arrival, we of
the interminable skid... Mr.

P sat in the backseat, bunched with
  everyone else. "Please, please,
    Mr. P," I said looking back
                          as
  we began to swerve… Swerved
  and spun and we pulled into
  Los Gatos, back where the song
  began. In the dream I saw
                        we
  dreamt our way there… Silly
as that, dream-silly, Mr. P met
  Mr. DJ. Silly as that, we pulled
                          in,
  1971… I sat in a room spin-
ning discs, an impromptu Taoist,
  again where the Andoumboulou
                            first
beckoned, smoke wafting the brunt
  of our dismay… Bailed out by
  dreaming, awoke back where
                        we
  were… We lay on stretchers,
                        para-
  medics toted us
  away

———————————————

Chthonic adornment lay
to our right, lyricless music,
an old soul's love we'd
have known… A man alone
in
Lisbon, solito we'd have
said in Spain, careen in
the car though we might
we
sang, orphans no matter
which way… The chorus
lay underground, chthonic
murmur, chronic insistence
not to
subside it
seemed

OLDTIME ENDING

for Ed Roberson, Ted
Pearson & Fred Moten

Reluctant light light's
evasion, faces lit. Soulin'
  one of them called it,
                        they
  sat around the fire… Re-
  ticulate eyelight, life
outliving childhood…
  Bottomless whimsy,
                        bot-
  tomline wisp… All atop
time running out, what
  the attendant buzz was,
                        gleam
  seen somewhere else,
  anyone else's eye… All
  to say they lay thrown out
of the car, sprawled at cliff's
                        edge.
  Their heads hit the dirt, they
  saw stars… It seemed they
saw love's low claw, rims
  riding asphalt, road their
                        dis-
  tended redoubt… Saw
  themselves thrown from
  the car, remembering
                        when,
  skin's old regard more
  skin… The end of it
  met the end of the world,
skid no out of which but
                        out,
  dead or passed out, un-
  seen outside face they fell
                        in-
  side

•

Their heads' hit of dirt
  launched feathers. The
boy-god with birdlegs
                    lashed
    out… A made-up
tribe's tale of the tribe it
  was they were caught
in, careened against all
                    hope
of coming thru but came
  thru. Moot consequence…
Moody surmise… "If any-
  one should ask what
                    this
was," the what-sayer sang,
  "say it was one for the
road the road rejected, some-
    thing for Ed that Ed
                    might
  have said, something for
  Ted that Ted might've
said, something for Fred
                    that
  Fred might've said, any-
thing should anyone ask…"
  So went the oldtime ending,
                    un-

  ending. *Something for*
  _____ *that* _____ *might've*
  said echoed *something*
for _____ *that* _____
                    might
  have said echoed *some-*
thing for _____ *that* _____
  might've said, echoed
                    with-
  out end or
amen

Stories told wanting to
be where they pointed...
   Flames they sat encircling
telling tales... The telling
                    come
  to no end, they sat listen-
   ing, flame-obsessed, ears
blown on by the wind...
  What was it the singing
                   said,
   they kept wondering.
 Something about a crash,
   they thought... That the
what-sayer sang smoked
                out
  certainty, they were un-
   sure. Something about
rescue, they thought...
                No
  sooner thought than it
  was time to get going.
Trip City loomed outside
               the
   woods' theoretic rest,
  bait they were bent on
              reach-
 ing that much
more

•

"A madman at the wheel,"
   they heard him whisper,
   the boy-god's low-key
   invective to no avail.
                     Rocked
      from side to side, put
   upon by chaabi, a madman
   at the wheel beyond a
                        doubt...
      Rocked from side to
   side, a boat it might've
   been, the birdlegged boy
   its masthead had it been, a
                        slur
      pulled at the side of his
   mouth. This the ythmic
   trek to Trip City: car
   no metaphor, inveterate skid
                        no
      allegory, the ditch they
   ended up in literal, every-
   thing resolute, real... So
   they thought or so they
                        said
      they thought. Thought
   disputed it. Mr. P's law
   was that thought would
                        have
      none of it. So much of
   what they said they thought
   thought refuted, Mr. P's
                        ac-
   complice, they complained...
   No sooner that than the
   skid they thought endless
   ended. No sooner that
                        as
      though complaint made it
   so... An increased im-
   munity came over them, what-

said cover, thought's
                    qualm
and rebuff, cover's what-
said complaint… Cover's
whatsaid compliance it was,
                    what-
ever worked worked out ad
hoc… The tale's torn cloth
what all there was of it,
the tale the tale's rending,
                    not
enough. They awoke some
other morning on some
other side of morning, happy
                    to
awake but happy-sad to be
awake, unsure they were awake,
surprised… They were get-
ting to be chagrined again. No
                    one
could say what they made
of it, road gone from as it
was, awoke from what…
Sprawled in what was known
                    as
aftermath, light's disguised
arrival, light's abject ad-
dress… Light looking into
                    which
they could only squint, go
off the road where the
highway bent… That was
                    the
way the story
went

THE OVERGHOST OURKESTRA
PLAYS FOR LOVERS

—"mu" eighty-second part—

A nonsonant ensemble
the two of them, athwart
  morning, morning's
                    dis-
  array... With little
time left, wondered were
  they alive enough.
  Steeped in dissimula-
  tion, heads each a
                    beat-
  en box, no sooner
  there than on their
  way out it seemed
                    of
late... Her his new and
  old Anuncia, slight
of chest but with bur-
  geoning hips, his
                    kryp-
tonite. Weakness, nemesis,
                              myth...
  Him her Trip City escort,
  rusted nails for hair,
head a cracked pepper,
  sweetness's defeat. Mot-
  ley roost, all the birds
                    of
  the world atweet where
                              his
  legs met, he of the stiff
demand her hand finessed...
  Soft cloth draping cleft
                    and
  protuberance... Calamitous
  lip lingered on and hung
from, kissed, better to've
  beaten back decline. Bro-

ther and Mrs. Vex they
                              now
  were, late of Stick City,
  Brother and Mrs. Vex
almost umbilical, back to
                              back,
  belly to back, belly to belly...
  They heard strings, Hofri-
yati thread, nonsonant though
                              they
  were. Marionettes they might
  have been, puppet stuff,
  shadow play projection,
                              scruff.
Soon-come concord the non-
    sonance theirs announced,
    tugged on, toyed with, lifted
                              up,
    dropped... A nonsonant
  symphony it might've been,
  nonsonant sound track, a
nonsonant bossa nova backing
                              the
  movie they felt they were in,
  strung lips meet without mu-
  sic though they did, lips' a
                              cap-
  pella itch never
quit

They were Mrs. Vex and Mr.
Fret but on the box "Me
and Mrs. Jones." 1972 it
    might've been... *The*
                    Black
Saint and the Sinner Lady
    followed, "Solo Dancer."
Time leaned in, no matter
                    when
    it might've been. 1963
    it might've been... Swank
    refrain said to've been
about sex, bodily blare,
    lyricless though it was
                    none-
    theless... Nonsonance the
    name it got, otherwise word-
    less, band say nothing
                    or
    it all amount to nothing,
    punctual only punctual,
                    noth-
    ing add
    up

•

Sound as disassembly it
seemed, a feast of in-
decency as though they
                    were
    a feast of indecency,
    thrust and the letting
    of limbs as though
                    they
were that... Wrapped
    herself in the frayed
    cape he wore, "Rag
        Sonata" the track
                    they
    heard had there been
one, wish though they
    might that there be
                    no
    preconception, no be-
        fore brunt their thrill...
Bodily allure the world
    they were leaving sound
                    in-
    sisted, nonsonant remove
    sound's inference, thrust
and the letting of limbs...
                    Their
    wish was thus they'd be
    alive again, band in back
        of them loud with
                    new
    power, nonsonance's nonce
    abatement, hot moment
                    they'd
    be bond-
ed by

Had found themselves
furthered unbeknown
to themselves. They
heard chatter in back
                        of
the wall behind the
backdrop, beyond
in-back more of the
same... Exit ran
                        into
and out of it, ad-
vance and retreat, his
and hers with or
                        with-
out

Mrs. Vex and Mr. Fret's tale
  regaled us. Unlikeliness's
allure we'd become converts
                    to
  of late, readiness and reluc-
    tance's draw... A continent's
  width away from Lone Coast
                  we
came to Low Forest, reminisced
  what never was. Called it soul,
  not knowing what soul was, as
                  if to
  say we'd have otherwise known...
  In Low Forest we got dirt under
                    our
    nails. The Overghost Ourkestra
  blared out of earshot, bass light
    spangled with leaf glint, glimmer,
                      we
    scrounged on the forest floor...
  It was a weighty sound, soon-come
  somnolence, work to remain awake
    though we did. A plumb sound it
                    was,
  nonsonance notwithstanding, heavy
    sound we sensed on our hands and
knees... It was a voyage we were on
                  un-
    der house arrest. Nod lay in front
  as though flown from inside, gone
    from reminiscence's ramshackle
auspices, ransacked romance's house.
                      Dis-
  mantling it, we stood, stewed, steadied
    ourselves as we could. Low Foresters...
Foragers...   Found our legs...

  Seeing we could stand, we sat. An
  organ quartet arrested us. San Fran-
  cisco, 1971, it seemed we were in,

Jack's on Sutter Street. We sat on
                                    logs
    encircling a fire, telling tales...
  Rooms under the ground amplified
  what sound there was, wood we
                                sat
ensconsed in, hollow what else there
                                    was...
    We came to see or it came to seem
  Nod lay behind us, long since rickety
    exit, rickety floorboards under our
  feet. Thus it was or so we said it went,
                                      Mrs.
  Vex and Mr. Fret's ythmic boon by
    the wayside, soon-come croon, com-
  plaint... Memory Lane it might've
                                  been
    but we were bent on the moment,
  Nuff the arch name it got, always
                                  never
  enough

What with Brother and Mrs.
Vex departed, what with knowing,
what with what could not be
happening happening, we moved

on...

Low Forest lay east of Detroit,
north of New Not Yet. Toward
the upcoming slope we saw sparkle,

calm

we called reckoning, Nuff... Look
back in advance we'd have none
of, did so even so. Somewhere
judges whispered into their

robes...

Someone had said or somewhere

we'd

read the stars were campfires farther
out. Pilgrims orbited each of
them, we'd heard or we'd read

some-
where

•

Calm we called reckoning, desire-
less we'd become. Up thru the roof
we went, angry. "Want, be ours
                                                            a-
gain," we grumped... Shook
our heads, pulled our hair, saw
something shine, not knowing
                                                    what.
Light's next-to-last will and what-
say. Fractal respite. Fractal un-
rest... We stole away from it,
    heads each a cocoon hatching
                                                    ap-
petite, long since lapsed arousal,
    erstwhile rouse, regret... There was
a bag we'd forgotten to watch and
                                                    some-
one had stolen. Reprimand spiked
    love's potion, love's dream lost
love clung to, clasp it all advancing
                                                    fell
away from, time intolerant, intan-
gible, touch and go... We were
    loss's intimates, inmates, wings
    unfurled inside the cocoons our
                                                    heads
had become. Not so, we said when
someone said we were dreaming.
    Naked, someone said. Not so,
                                                    we
said... A dialogue of soul and sex
    it had been but shifted, the what-
    sayer adamantly back. What to
do, what of what comes after, he
                                                    was
    asking, Mr. P's confidante... A
dialogue of soul and subsequence,
    what was debated what would be.
                                                    A
grandmother strangling a water snake

114

in Georgia was all the history, he
said, he knew… So it was we learned
                                    of
    social burlap, divination's rough cut,
        the what-sayer claiming to've dined
    with the President. Pitch, provocation,
                                        boast…
        We were love's last portion, politics
                                        our
    stretch, nowhere not orexic still. Again
    we'd go the way of new Andoumboulou,
    large heads turbaned with butterfly wings,
                                        co-
        coons they'd truly turn out to've been…
    The what-sayer's date with the President
    cracked us up. Mr. and Mr. Plex we'd
                                        have
    said. We applauded Nub's facelift, ballot-
        box pendulum, wondered without asking
        what next… We stood in the parking
                                        lot
    Low Forest had morphed into, a remote
        lot Itamar had met his first love in. Asphalt
    stuck to our feet… We fended off sorrow,
                                        the
        earth awash in oil, black planet, a sigh so
                                            light
        feathers felt like
    lead

The parking lot might have been
a drive-in movie, so loosely did its aspect
fit. The what-sayer said they'd gone
to dinner even so, insisted it again
                                    and
        again... They'd eaten popcorn,
    rabbit and arugula, he said, meant by
        that to make us think. The sky
balled up in qu'ahttet light, Itamar
                                    said
        so too, the Overghost Ourkestra
gone but for a tremor, David S. Ware
        on the box... Love's graduation
                                        gone
    haptic, a poultice made of cardamom
        husks... Mr. and Mr. Plex fled pomp,
        ceremony, make-believe's long
                                    day
    done

•

Once again we thought of mov-
ing on, Low Forest a lid on
what we could see. Desireless
    but for that, owned a conceit
                                of
    sorts, wanting to be wise to
itself…Looking to leave part
    regret, part glee to be done
    with it, a little of it made its
                            way
back… A night out, a night not
    unlike others, drudgery's night
                                off
    at least. Yes, it was a drive-in
    movie, *The Tingler*, 1959.
We sat each with an ostensible
    mate and held hands, turned
                            away
    when it came to the scary parts…
We begged Mr. and Mr. Plex
    let go, cinegenic precedent
                            pest.
    Fog rolled in from the coast
    but only in memory, the
screen we sat in our cars looking
                            at
    obscured… Black hold, gnostic
hostages again, stellar collapse…
    Backlit galactic tarpit, spasmodic
                                as-
phalt we stepped in… It might've
    been a play we were staging.
I lent the cast what I felt, what was
    left of me, the reed's voice not
                            out
    of earshot, what sound could ac-
    crue to ennui. "We were dead
before we knew it," said the dead,
                            I
    heard it clearly. A quick wind

rose and was gone… The edge
I'd sworn we stood on retreated.
The nay's whoosh lamented the
                          mo-
ment as it faded, lament the sole
                          mo-
ment there was… The nay's lament
gave time a sound. Sad but okay
it seemed and so the dead said.
                          "We'll
be okay," they said… We was
a vain wish to rescue, Ahtt En-
semble the name it got… Ahtt was
an abstract aggregate. Hallelujahs
                          went

up as we pulled
out

     We knew no other way to say
it, so messed up we were. Mr.
  and Mr. Plex fled pomp, cere-
mony, eked-out amenity what
                                cast
  we could salvage, light's late
   show our chagrin… We
were light's last addicts, we
  feasted on frame, flicker,
                         the
  what-sayer's presidential
   fare our tale of the tribe,
                    light's
  last advocates,
lost

Listen to the reed-flute, how it complains,
Lamenting its banishment from its home.

—Rumi, *Masnavi*

SONG OF THE ANDOUMBOULOU: 104½

A loud Memnonian crack
   sang transience. High
lapsarian wind. Night
    pressed my ear to the
                reed's
   complaint… I saw no
light but light assaulted
    me it seemed. I dreamed
   a dream of going home,
               home
   gone, erstwhile we, loath
              to see
  it so, saw it
  so

SOUND AND SUPPLEMENT

—"mu" eighty-fourth part—

Toulali's desert voice lay
behind us, sanded cords
  we picked up in Tetuan.
Bossa nova's gnostic
            sigh
  had its way now, Na-
ra Leão was on the box
as we pulled out… Come
  the end what will it've
                been
  about, we wondered…
There not knowing why,
  we moved on… "World,
            be
  window, be wing," we
cried, "dipped in medicinal
  water we'd be," cried might
                cry
  make it so… Stunned polity's
  body absconded with, come
to grief before we could say,
             "Run
  come." South of stay, we
turned east in our extremity,
  bodily breakdown, spirit's
lament… God had a gun or
            was
  a gun someone shouted,
we ducked and ran. Soon-
come scatter. Scut… We to
  be a party again, appetite be-
  tween, wished-for civic
            remit.
Remnant kiss, tongue rum-
  maging teeth, gums, tongue,
  intimate spit's bouquet…
            Said

to've been inspired, said to've
                              been
    august, upstart avatar's we we
    might've been, run-come we
      we bumped up… The reed's
    voice had rubbed us raw, we
                              bare-
ly had skin left, lithe, insinuant
    blow a kind of sand, reed's
deep coo and complaint… What
                              blew
    thru made us wonder was what
    there was all there was. Either
                              it
    was unreal or the world was,
    a kind of salt it so burned as
                              it
blew

                    •

    Itamar's Maghrebi transport
calmed us. It was he the reed
    spoke thru, blown by no one
                              we
      knew, he whose discourse it
    drove… All would resolve,
      it said, sand buffed our faces.
We looked into the wind. Our
                              skin
      glowed… Yes, it was Itamar's
        talk, we told ourselves, Ita-
    mar's reel, no sweat… Outer
      body's inner body suspense
                              we
      disquisited. Choristers against
    our will, we heard our voices
        break, wooed by Itamar's
                              locu-
    tion, caroling ready or not… As
    if we'd be reeds to be blown

on, sopranino chatter, chirp... Sang
                              thru
    holes in our teeth, sucked wind
                         in,
   sopranino giggle,
grit

Sopranino grimace, grin. A
giant's eye it might've been
looked in on us, Persian
                          minia-
tures we might've been…
    So said the nay, could say
be said to apply. We were
trying not to mimic the
                          wind…
    "I, for one," I kept saying,
dreamt I said and kept saying,
                          intent

    not to mimic
    the wind

　　　　　•

　　Sweet pantied lips it put
　　its nose to, "mu" as in
　　musk. She's letting me
take them off, the nay
　　　　　　　　dreamt,
　　letting me alight upon
　　hair, waft what's un-
　　derneath…Who'd have
　　　　　　　　thought
　　the reed would speak that
　　way I drew back wondering,
　　arabesque loquat canopy
　　　　　　　　above,
　　　love's no longer lofty
　　redoubt… It was a tree
　　at whose base rotting fruit
　　lay. Reed was out of its ele-
　　ment I thought… All the
　　　　　　　　same
　　I heard it semising, semisay,
　　　all would be light and
　　love be its leige, lief to low
　　　　　　　　squat's
　　regress… It was the same old
　　saw, repeatedly remembered
　　　perfume where legs met,
　　　　　　　　hot
　　sun's adamance mixing
　　　bloom with sweat, the same
　　long song's old saw… It
　　　　　　　　was
the same long saw, sometimes
　　to be said only the old way.
　　It was one of many trees in
　　the plaza, one of only six
　　　　　　　　lo-
　　quats. We'd been circling
　　　for who knows how long,
　　driven around and around,

125

found it finally. "Mokhalef
                    Segah"
had come on the box as we got
    there. Muhammed Musavi
  escorted us in... "Ay Cariño"
                        came
    on next, Tito Puente, Santos
  Colón. Words were spirits
    the way they welled up with
  breathing, floated, palaver, pale
                        remit.
    In love with pendency, immi-
  nence, portending, wooed by
    the about-to-be, the not-yet...
  Outside the recital room our
                        heads
    had become nay meant
  negation, waft and what lay
  underneath rescinded, song's
    meek polity rebuked...
                        Our
    Lady of the Loquat Tree we
    dreamt anyway, Our Lady's
                        quick
    spread and dis-
  play

———————————

"No civic remit, no pantied
epiphany," Itamar said the
    nay proclaimed. "Body-part
                                    muse
    my bad…" Again the shout
God had a gun or was a gun,
    again shots rang thru the
air… We were trying to make
                                    sound
    our solace, bullets punctured
it, trying to make sound our
    haven, bombs exploded,
trying to make heaven home…
                                    All
    a vain wish, whimsy, wind,
    blown hope wanting not
to mimic the wind… Naysaid
                                    re-
    mit, "My
bad"

Next up we parked our bus in
a cul-de-sac, called it a day.
Naysay's conjure lay behind us,
   nothing stirred. Being dead
               will
  be like this we thought...
  Sound and supplement fell
away and we as well. It was
  our time to be upset... Tales
             of
  outrage regaled us now,
    trumped-up fire we camped
around. There was a life not
             the
one we were living, dreams
    lined up, we knew, no end...
  Lapsed moment not gotten
            back
we thought utopic, thought's
  fare now something we ran
from, thought's fare not
  something at all... We
           aban-
doned our book of the
    immaculate moment, book
of Our Lady's pantied rump...
  All was anger and we were
           an-
gry, gruff throats packed with
          saw-
  dust, no such thing as we'd
have said we
saw

        •

We walked like pilgrims not-
withstanding we sat, circling
  the fire we sat around raging...

The kingdom of the loquat
                    seed
    lay around the bend, bullet
    and bomb's day soon
done. It was all bend, we
                    went
    around and around, not
        getting around it. The logs
were loquat branches, leaves,
                    lo-
    quats and all... Trumped-up,
        the logs were unreal. We
    teased it out as we walked
                    a-
    round in circles, erstwhile
        epiphany, made-up lament,
        glimpse we got it might be only
                    that...
    Made-up religion was all it was,
        made-up amends, gun-glad
Church of Saint Angry, made-up
    arrest athwart the moment's
                    de-
    mise... We wept, so entropic
    it was, hands, even so, balled
    into fists. We were Nub's
polyphonic nonsemble, clumps
                    of
    noquats in our hands as we
    sat circling, Nub's new council
                    of
no

＿＿＿＿＿＿＿＿＿

Say-it-again said it again.
Someone said we were in
China. The reed orange
hovered above… We were
                              con-
    fused was it fruit or the
promise of fruit we wanted,
    concealment or display
or display of concealment,
                              for-
    ever to be on the verge of
      being shown… We were
    upset something more
                              we
    could've had went by un-
      gotten, the one something
                              not
    something
    at all

ANABATIC RING SHOUT

—"mu" eighty-sixth part—

    Rings were the new yoga,
new and old yoga, out the
  tighter they got, in again
                                 out…
    I sat circling the wax in my
head, candlelit stutter step I
  dragged myself thru, stiff-
legged shuffle, shout… I
                       sat
  circling a blown-out candle,
                           black
  wick. Argument heated my
head… Flame blacked my
  head's insides, my familial
dead no longer dead, alive
                         again.
    All of them drunk, still
dying of thirst, not yet dead
  again, my aunt fell into
the stereo, the others followed
                          suit…
  The Three Sounds played in
the background, *Black Orchid*,
  "Tadd's Delight." The
                    outer-
  most province of loop it was,
cartoon solace what condolence
  there was… I dragged a leg
                    cir-
  cling the thought of it, burnt
                      wick
  where the record was, so abject,
  so out of place, it might've
been Mu we came there from…

  Muddy Waters was up next
  in the background, the one

something the same thing
                              sung
    about, the new something
new again and again. I sat
    circling, Muddy's eyebrow
the sun I revolved around, the
                              sun's
    late arcade fell away... Blue
                              trudge,
    blue faraway lumen. Blue grip
an aggrieved inkling, moment's
    not-knowing, late lullaby of
                              not-
    know. All to insist we'd only
        of late begun listening, chicken
bones piled on the kitchen counter,
    all the saints turned out in badly
                              fit
    shoes... I sat wincing, it hurt
                              so
    to see them hobble, bunions
    relieved by slits cut in their Stet-
    sons, bunions, ingrown toenails,
                              corns...
All the same I sat listening, legs tucked
    under, spinning in the middle of
                              the
    air. Taken away, I meant to say, not
tucked, ground gone out from under,
    my other aunt's amputated legs. The
                              I
    that was, then the I that wasn't,
    I sat circling in-between... Ring
my deciduous yoke, my bound
                              exit,
    ring my sometime release. Ring
    was the new and old yoga. I sat
                              want-
    ing off the
wheel

One thing I could say about
ring was as it went around I
   felt uprooted. Ring was all
I knew if I knew anything,
                              aco-
   lyte of not-know of late…
   Circling, put upon by he,
she, they and we, Itamar, Mrs.
P, all the pronouns, all the
                              names,
   Anuncio and Anuncia not
the least. I wasn't Anuncio
   but felt I was, Anuncia's
                              hip
   against his his would-be
                              world
   without end, thigh rolled up
on thigh, heavenly her atop
   him… Nut she might've been
or he'd have had her tease,
                              pre-
   tend, there but not there, grudging
   intimate, blasé abandon, re-
mote. Her faraway look he'd
                              have
   seen up close, offhand inti-
mate, nose dilated more by
   her own smell than his, re-
luctance their upstart muse…
                              Nut
   she might've been, arced over
   him, loin musk opening her
nose but uncommitted, above it
                              all,
   Egyptian sky…It was the rim
of the well or the ring of the
   world. The well of the ring
                              it
   might've been… Thought after
   thought after thought, arc in

all of them, Nunca's abstract
be-
hind his hands grabbed at,
reaching past the one that was
there... Ring's farthest reach
of mind it might've been.
Round and round, mindless,
I
went... I wore lensless wirerim
specs,
closed my eyes, not to see what
he saw, so put upon I was, not
to see him and her looked at...
They were the same, Andoum-
boulou, in each other's face,
faces
where their legs met, neither
knowing up from down. Ring
was helical shout, the hill
they went up and down, all its
choric
urgency theirs again, not to
know so they might have
their way, their gambit, shed their
regret, have their shot... A
dawn-
ing sound they wanted but
dark and without corolla, solace
at their beck, they thought, tugged
from under them, a forwarding
they
felt taken back... They felt the
verge they were on, the welling
up, the wet lid, noquat lift and
relinquishment, verge they wanted
wiped
away

•

They'd walked in circles
holding signs, up with this,
  down with that, dream their
suzerainty the slogan said. A
                       slow
  dervish it wasn't but was, a
  demonstration, a protest
in love's republic, love no
  republic yet... Mind at large,
                      feet
  following, home where whim
took them, newly named Fasa,
  strewn since who could say
                   when,
  sought city farther off than
God... The glad work of
  getting there they called it,
no matter how grim they
                were,
  peripatetic stress of blood
what there was of it, mind un-
  attached, feet hemorraging,
               blown
  grit peppering their skin...
Around and around they
  went holding placards, cir-
cling some lack they protested,
             Nub's
  embassy undone... It wasn't
  Nub's collapse or lost money
they were mourning, elegiac
            birth-
  right's lurch and repercussion,
  it wasn't as attributable as
             that...
Blue sky lay above, ostensible
  benefice, Nut's light disguise
            they
  thought

A subdued cry caught in
   their throats leaked out, breath
packed in cracks in dry mud...
    It wasn't Zar they were in
                          but
   it might've been, Dread Lakes
   diaspora they'd come thru
they thought, nothing no matter
                        where
   they looked, flat cabinet, heaven's
    cracked integument coming
    down... Glimpse and departure
                    love's
   currency they'd read, each the
    other's alternate book, lids heavy,
                      the
   look they gave going
 away

•

One thing I could say about
ring was as it came around I
  said keep out of it, the we or
                       the
  would-be we truly them, no
tune lifted my feet… There
  was the world I reminded
myself, Nub's new entropy
                     not
  to be dismissed, I nursed a
low moan in my throat. Leaflets
  and confetti came down from
                     the
  clouds, rain the ushering
horns would have none of, trom-
  bones bolted my feet at ring's
edge, the one thing I could
                  say
  stuck to my tongue… Ring
                  was
  none other than rung, low
brass expounded, lift I'd not
  be given to. I gathered my
anguish in a bag, sucked wind
                 and
  hiccupped, coughed and
coughed again, coughed up
              straw…
  Rung's doubling back, dou-
bling's bolt it seemed it was,
  orbit arbiting light it might've
              been.
  Orbit arbiting light was another
Nub was all I could see, Anuncio
  and Anuncia Quag's two backs…
              So
  it was the one thing I could say
was more than one, unspun am-
  biguous witness, wound unecstatic

stump… Antiphonal whimsy why
                                              they
    were so up and me reluctant, fist
    in my chest, remote, low brass's
        consort, contrapuntal straw
        coughed up… The concept slid
                                              and
    we slid with it, weeping wrung one
        with sweat. Wizened voices' rough
    concupiscence, toll and tolling's
                                              es-
    cort, the chorusing horns' condo-
    lences glum… We made a game
                                              of
        it, parallactic hub to ring's rim,
        rung's perimetric slough. The
    concept slid and came back and
                                              we
        came with it. Not to get one's
        hopes up I warned and the horns
        also, also and as much and all
                                              the
    more

But my second body said
otherwise. Visitor from planet
   Whiff, gnostic doorpeep,
sniffed an imagined musk
                              where
      there was none, lived in
   what let hope have its way…
      My second body put off
   by body one's complaint
                              said
      not so. The one thing I
      could say was more than
      one, my second head said,
                                    first
         head's hard reflex not all
         there was of it, first head's
                                          boast
      and re-
   buff

I was love's own distant
lover, first body and first
head I kept at bay. First
                    body,
    one foot at ground level,
walked with a hitch, the
    other foot underground…
Be sold on hope, it seemed
                            I
    heard Sophia say. Why
sold I wondered, quick to
    correct. Be souled on
    hope, Sophia said…
                        Rung
    was to rim as ring was
    to rut. My second body
                        leapt
    and leapt
on

LOW FOREST ROTATION

—*"mu"eighty-eighth part*—

Again we set out somewhere
else, we the migrating they their
    bent antennas, they who in
                        love's
    mind saw themselves. It was
love's first mind they saw
    themselves in, outset's
luminous musk incumbent,
                        never
    not there they thought…
    They sat still in their second
bodies looking, love's first
                        mind
    a resplendent window, blue
    sky bright birds flew thru…
We the migrating they talismanic,
    parallactic they to ourselves…
                        Par-
allax meant panorama, glimpsed
    adjacency hub tore loose toward,
                        ten-
    uous body what vantage there
    was. We were nothing if not
        head, nothing if not body, first,
second, third, fourth, further… We
                        were
    nothing if not pull between first
    and second body, book to
    second's opening first would
                        be…
    Cleft emanation second body
was, rip, lytic whatsee, inside
    come to light, lyric bent so
much what we were but not the
                        half
    of it, we the migrating they's
    dispatch… Pull between one

and the next body. Book to
                              sub-
    sequent opening body would
                              be.
    Clash the one thing that spoke
      though speech abounded, song's
    auspice also, meaning drawn out...
                              Could
      we only be theirs or be there, we
        lamented, all would be ours
    again... It was theirs to come get
    us, we said, ours to be gotten,
                              came
      to where we were and at last
    were all there and all was as it
      was again... Thus the one wish,
                              the
      one we were held by, never put
    to rest or not yet put to rest, walked
      with a box on our head we called
                              home,
      box more hat than
    home

We were each caught with a
box on our head we called a
house, hat more than house
though it was. A houseboat
                          we'd
have had it, pinegreen waters
                              the
trees underneath, John Canoe
namesake boat, Junkanoo head-
dress, boat more than box we
thought… In our second minds
                            we
saw our second heads floating,
Junkanoo dreadnoughts' chro-
matic armada… Note not to go
out on, paperweight imbroglio,
                        fight's
fly-by auspices'
arrest

Centrifugal egress, rut we swung
away from... Ripped eccentric
fabric, Junkanoo cloth... It was
                                  the
slaves' day off and we worked
it, secondhead sweat's new
day soon come, firsthead misery
ceased... We were beside our-
selves, arms out like wings,
                                  low
to the ground, Junkanoo jets it
seemed. Fighter jets, dreadnoughts,
weapons for the weaponless,
                                  mili-
tia to end militias, mother of all
militias, we the migrating they's
millenarian swat... Wound it as
we would and rework it, the world
                                  lay
in convalescent light. Wound it
as we would and fall away con-
vinced, all was as it was again,
                                  cir-
cular, pine trees washed in burnt
orange umbra, all come to itself
come back to itself, beginning's
                                  be-
ginning again... The Bahamas
had nothing to do with it, think
Junkanoo though we did, but
did have to do in that everything
                                  did,
nothing if not eclectic, ecumeni-
cal, the everything everything was...
So again we were athwart where
                                  we
were, the elsewhere whose hum love
tethered, boxheaded emigrants the we
antennas fell from, no known fre-

quency's cue. Wound it as we would
                              we'd
have none of it, made-up armistice ours
to insist. Wound as we would, world
would out... I wanted to stop and say
                                stop.
    I wanted world-would-out taken
                                back.
    Wheel whose whir drowned hum out,
    love's telepathic straw, I wanted to
say stop, we messed up... I was the
    wheel I wanted spun, microcosmic
                                ratch-
    et, grain the machine's gear bumped
up. As were we all, each at a time, it
    wasn't real. It was ritual we were
lost in, would-be ritual, would-be lost,
                                Low
    Forest Mass manqué... It was a mess.
    I said stop, we messed up. Everyone
in turn said the same. Say stop though
                                we
    did we didn't stop. Outset's earthy per-
fume filled our noses, we the migrating
    they's wounded prospects, wound as

                                we
    would, moved on... Love's labyrinth
    itself we were in, Junkanoo hats
on our heads that were houses, houses
    that were boats that flew... Low Forest
                                lay
    all around us. On toward the heart's
own City we trekked, City we'd heard
    lay west of us, we the migrating likeness
                                we
saw

Pine-branch batons fell into
their hands as they walked, a
    relay of sorts they were in.
                        Gate
to the eventual City, woodland
    rampart, apart from where
    they were though they were...
                        First
    head's hiccup, second head's
    expanse, trudge though they
        would, sweet nativity's tele-
metry, nativity their resolute
                        wish...
    Ta'wil where they'd be, it
    was their manyheaded exegete,
                        soul's
        own home it
    seemed

In soul's memory doffed hats
that were houses. Stood bone
 close, a relay of sorts… Love's
                               first
   mind found out were life longer,
  dream they kept dreaming,
                          love's
    republic lived in, all but all
                              there,
    trudged
    on

We took to the road, Wagadu
revisited, more times fallen asleep
than we could count. "Were
                                        all
   as we would want," we re-
minded ourselves, the we that
   we were on our way toward...
All else behind, Wagadu no
                              way,
   Baltimore it was we were in.
   Baltimore it was, then Cincin-
nati, stone buildings meant to
mean forever, squat stone stacked
   against time... So it was away
                                        was
   all there was of it, it the inside
we were after, not there where
   we were or not there when we
were, said to've been there but
                                        gone...
   Second bodies carried us far-
ther. We were truly blue Fasa
   now. *Live at the Apollo* was
                              on
   the box and we sang along,
                                        each
   the Apollonian someone we
sang about, lost Apollonian some-
   one, second body we lagged be-
hind... We the Andoumboulou,
                                        we
   the blue Fasa, we the hurt com-
mencement whose hurt kept rip-
   pling, we the ones who thought of
                                        them
   still

     •

     Outside Cincinnati it got green
  again. The river and the river
   valley went on forever, idyllic
outside the knots inside our
               vehicle,
    Itamar calling Sophia his
  "gnostic hottie" not the least…
   We rode along, we measured
             our
    dismay, we audited the life
  whose allegory our wandering
    was, Itamar called Sophia
his "gnostic hottie" again and
           again,
    straddling another life it seemed.
   "Cheeks each the size of my
hand," he muttered trancelike,
   lost and remembering it seemed…
Flown moment he lamented gone
          again,
    on we rode. Sophia kissed her
  fingertip, shushed him, blushed a
   little it seemed… So spoke the
lamented moment outside the bubble
           we
    were otherwise in, moment's gnosis
    moving on agreed with, broken
   moment sophic moment flowed
from… The short while we could
         all
    be there was all we wanted. There
  wasn't anything we were after
         any-
more. It all flew by, a blur of green,
   brown and blue, unintruded on
by this or that somewhere, whatever
         else-
    where we were leaned on by… The
  life whose allegory our wandering
   was was ours again, each element

its own leave, its own legend, itself
                              said
    of itself… No recondite itinerary's
    dictates hurried us. It was what
it was, one was tempted to say but
    bit one's tongue… What Itamar
                                   call-
    ing Sophia his "gnostic hottie"
    had lit subsided, her eyes big with
      him in them no longer a glimpse
                                   into
    another life… Hurtling past the stars
      had it been a rocket we were in, our
                                   van

    fluxing green, brown and
    blue

Ohio fell away, we traveled
east heading west, lost tribe
known by name alone. We
                              came
    to ridge after ridge after ridge,
an impending world inside the
    one we were in, Steal-Away
                              Ridge
    long since left behind...
    "Going forward" lay on every-
    one's lips, wishful, a wand
we waved, would-be wand,
                              in-
    sistent, spell we'd have cast
                              if we
    could

•

We of the book the book's blue
fascicle, a new pact between name
and not knowing, rag, tatter,
                              rav-
    ening bundle, raveling thread.
Bundled incense, neroli's plumb
funk, we smelled of the east...
                              At
no point on any map, at all points on
    every map. So went the doctrine
                              we'd
read... It was an ode to the nth self
    and soul our ride rang changes on,
                              bled
        undercoat's blue primer painted
        over, a coat of many colors we
        wanted to say... "World," we want-
    ed to say, "be palette, moot polity,
                              move-
        ment's pretend purity, ruse, un-
        rest." "World," we said instead,
                              "be
    still," not meaning it, Nub's pleo-
        nastic rut... Something one of us
had read had hold of us, questions
    answers jammed. Said, it seemed a
                              stick
        bodily breakdown wielded, a boon
        albeit none of us knew why, anagogic
        baton... It was the book of erasing
                              the
book the book attached us to, rub as we
    did or would, due dissepiment, light
    blue blank our dissolve. A movie it
                              oc-
    curred we were in, strewn amplitude,
    third, fourth, fifth embattlement, to be
                              to be
        at odds it
seemed

Sophic moment more move than
moment, a certain something's
  tug from inside… Something
                              seen
  in a face it seemed a world
    opened out from, love's
republic a real place it seemed…
  Second body's recollected
                              some-
    where. Said somewhere's
  arrested cachet… So many
    beads told, horsejaw interstice,
                              ride
    we told our horse
tell no

•

Came together a common wish
to make real. Truly pretend Fasa,
  pretense made us blue, made-up
                              An-
  doumboulou as well... Dystopic
    stent... Utopic huddle... It
was all a masque, a moving tableau.
What became of us back when,
                              we
  kept wondering, where were we
and what did the names we heard
    mean... *Bazoumana Sissoko
Live in Fallujah* was on the box,
                              it
  made us hum, tight strings
pinched and let go. A thin thread
  we hung by lifted us, the n'goni's
rattan rasp unlikely even so, hoisted
                              us,
  humming, we soared... So it was
we made it safely thru Peepshow
  Pass, moneyshot war report the
                              new
  breast and thigh. Our high Sahelian
    canto carried us. *Live in Kandahar*
was up next... We were secondheaded.
                              We
  each had no outer body. All was inside,
    undisclosed... A long heavenly road
  it would've been had it been ours to
                              say
  but there was no such getaway, no
  not being there. We were hungry ghosts,
    we rode farther east. We sat in back-
  seats eating ghosht, we were in India,
    bumped across Uttar Pradesh... How
                              far
  it was, we thought, far over, each an
  Insofar-I's host, guest, ghost, gone

so much as gotten there. It wasn't
we now knew what soul was. It wasn't
  Wagadu was near, it wasn't Ouadada…
                                    We
  ambled on, moist-eyed, refusing to cry,
stiff jaw set on second body's elysium,
  second body's long run come… We
                                ate
    ghosht, we sipped colonial sodas…
  We rode the Insofar-I's totem horse
    we traded bodies with, told it tell
my host as we rode. Mix though we
                              did,
    it wasn't there yet, the Vedic vodoun
      elixir we were after, Ital bedouin
  brew… At one of our stops I wan-
dered off alone, secondheaded even
                                    so,
    second body inside my first head
      it seemed, burnt-out factory, boarded-
up church. What Itamar had said he'd
                                    seen
    it seemed I saw, life whose allegory we
  were lost in, sophic fire, gnostic spark…
    I saw no light but what looking shed, I
                                      saw
    light, lightwheel spinning the size of a
  pin's head, secondheaded glimpse and
      gone… Came together a common wish
  to make real I remembered, third, fourth,
                                    nth
    head and body, third, fourth, nth remove
                                    or
    remit